Trinity Matters

In Faith, Work, and Love

… and Even Theology

STEVE DANCAUSE

This book is dedicated to my wife, Meredith. Your contributions to my life are beyond words.

"What you think about when you think about God shapes your imagination for community and for the good life. *Trinity Matters* teases this out profoundly! Steve Dancause has been exploring this great divine mystery for most of his years on this planet and now we get to join him in the wonder and joy of discovering abundant life in the Three and the One."

-Dr. Dwight J. Friesen
Associate Professor of Practical Theology at The Seattle School of Theology & Psychology. Co-author of *The New Parish*, *Routes and Radishes*, and author of *Thy Kingdom Connected*. Co-founder of the *Inhabit Conference* and *Leadership in the New Parish*.

TABLE OF CONTENTS

List of Illustrations   iv

1   The Painful Truth   7
Our Trinity Problem.

I. WHO MATTERS

2   Whom We're Talking About   11

3   When It Comes to Work, It's About the Who   15
Not the rock band. How the Trinity matters in our vocation.

4   Godless Christianity   18
We are uncomfortable with the paradoxes revealed by Jesus and prefer a watered-down Trinity. Three is a crowd, I guess.

5   And We Dance   22
Waltz? Tango? No. Perichoresis—the life of God in motion.

6   How Jesus Views Himself   26
The Trinity is our understanding because it is Jesus' self-understanding.

7   Parenting and Perichoresis   32
Parenting is proof that being God is hard work.

8   How the Church Came to Believe in the Trinity   35
And explain the Arian texts supporting subordination of the Son.

9   Who Should I Pray To?   41
I am tired of saying whom.

10   Sighting the Trinity   43
The double paradox of the Trinity and Jesus—illustrating who God is, and who God is not.

11   Every Century's Favorite Heresy   47
Arianism and subordinationism are popular, but they miss the point of Christianity.

12   The Holy Spirit Walks Into a Coffee Shop   51
Who is God, Spirit, and also a real person? The Holy Spirit.

13   Love, Right Thinking, and Other Religions   56
Can we get a little orthopraxy with our orthodoxy?

II. WHEN AND WHERE MATTERS

14 Butter, Jesus, and the Trinity 61
With apologies to vegans for this greasy analogy.

15 Putting Time and Space in Their Place 64
*Time and eternity are distinct, by definition and by God's design.
However, they come together as one in Jesus.*

16 I Need to Relate 72
*Jesus must be human to be relatable. Yet he must be God to bear
the weight of eternity.*

17 Temporal and Eternal "Trinities" 75
*The classical view is on its way out, yet it leaves us with dual "trinities"
and no one path to integration. The double paradox of Jesus is the key.*

18 God, Gender, and Common Humanity 80
The Trinity breaks through all barriers of division. We should too.

19 One Will or Three Wills? 85
The Garden of Gethsemane Question.

20 Jesus: The Problem and the Answer 88
*Jesus has always been a dilemma, as well as the solution to a God of
relationship.*

21 The Arian Reaction 93
Arianism—a logical response to the Jesus problem.

22 Time and Eternity in Jesus 96
A model illustrating a Christo-centric view of time and eternity.

23 Marriage and Mutual Submission 104
Reciprocal submission in love is God's example and command to us.

24 Theological Dilemmas 107
How to honestly have it both ways.

25 Jesus Is Lord of All 113
How the Son makes Christianity universally true.

III. HOW AND WHY MATTERS

26   God is Other-Centered   119
Bearing the imago Dei is a communal, other-centered activity.

27   The Model of the Actual Trinity   123
A dynamic, multi-directional perichoresis that incorporates the economy of salvation.

28   Agape and Hierarchy   130
Mutual submission is not identical relations.

29   Scripture and the Actual Trinity   134
The picture that Scripture draws for us: the mutual submission of the Trinitarian communion.

30   Taking Traditional Babies Out of the Bathwater   139
We can keep the traditional descriptions when we see them within the larger, subordination-free picture.

31   East and West—Having It Both Ways   143
Reconciling the Eastern and Western models.

32   Roles and Ranks   147
Why are you in charge?

33   The Great Invitation   152

APPENDICES

1   Four Hazards of Integration   157
Things to avoid in any integrative model of the Trinity.

2   Integrative and Egalitarian Models?   164
The triumphs and failings of the LaCugna and Jenson proposals, and requirements of a complete model.

3   Eternally Begotten?   172
There is no Scriptural support for the Son's begotten-ness.

4   What About Subjugation in 1 Corinthians 15:20-28?   176
It is really a picture of mutual submission.

5   How About All Those Sunday School Analogies?   178
They're all right. They could be righter.

Bibliography   183

LIST OF ILLUSTRATIONS

Figure	Page
1. The Double Paradox	20, 43
2. The Double Paradox With the Outer Rim	44
3. Eastern Trinities	78, 143
4. Western Trinities	78, 144
5.1. God, Eternity, and Time	96
5.2. God, Eternity, and Time	97
5.3. God, Eternity, and Time	98
5.4. God, Eternity, and Time	99
5.5. God, Eternity, and Time	101, 113
6. Disintegrated Theology	108
7. Integrated Theology	110
8. The Trinity—Integrated, Egalitarian, and Dynamic	123, 137
9. Combing the East/West, Eternal/Temporal Trinities	145
10. LaCugna Model	165
11. Jenson Model	168

ACKNOWLEDGMENTS

I would like to thank a few brave souls for suffering my many ideas and drafts over the years. This book would not have been possible without your criticism and encouragement.

Dwight Friesen, Hillary Bercovici, Micah Brickner, Ken Hoke, Trevor Spencer, Meredith Dancause—Thank you.

I would also thank Scott McFadden for the cover design, as well as Steve Kennedy, Cheryl Kennedy, Lauren Bennett and Mary Kaye Polacheck for copy editing.

Finally, my wife and daughter, who made many sacrifices in giving me the time to write this. Meredith and Imogen, thank you for helping me share this with the world.

1 THE PAINFUL TRUTH

Our Trinity problem.

It is commonly said that we don't fully understand the Trinity. This is true, but besides me, who cares? *Dozens of people*, my practically minded wife tells me. If you're one of them then this book is up your alley. The main work of this book will be to understand the Trinity better because it is necessary for the main point of this book—how the Trinity matters when it comes to life. That's what everybody wants to know. How does the Trinity matter in faith, work, and love? If we don't know, it is because we've lost the Trinity as the core of Christianity. The reason is not because we've left abstract theology behind, but rather because we have failed to keep Jesus, and his understanding of God—which includes himself—at the center.

If we don't deep down trust that Jesus is God alongside the Father, then why would we obey his commands? For example, why would we love our enemies—an extremely difficult thing to do—when it is easier to model our treatment of enemies on Old Testament passages that we find easier? And if we don't believe that the Holy Spirit is God alongside the Father and Son, then why would we submit to the Spirit's desire to transform us? We are indwelled by God himself, the Spirit within us, but it is difficult to imagine.

The painful truth is not that we don't understand the Trinity—though this is indeed painfully true—it's that we don't actually *believe* in the Trinity. And if we don't believe, then we don't put our weight on it and *act* as if it's true. The result is that we often fail to love as God loves. Belief in the Trinity goes hand in hand with discipleship. When we fail to believe, we fail to love, and thus we fail to evangelize to the world. After all, Jesus said that the world will know that we are his disciples by our love. I have become persuaded that what we believe about the Trinity matters.

The Church faces catastrophic decline in the developed West. Even in areas where some churches seem to be thriving, our general reputation is woeful. Why? Because we (the Church in Western society as a whole) don't follow the teachings of Jesus as paramount.

We prefer sectarian politics, sacred tribalism, legalism, academic philosophy, or a health-and-wealth gospel over a radical faith in Jesus who is God and perfectly reveals God's character. We have settled for weak views of the Trinity.

Most Christians think that the Trinity is confusing and impractical. On a personal level it just doesn't seem to matter. Those nerdy enough to care are led down philosophical rabbit holes that lead to little of value. This is a shame, for the Trinity is not only who God is, but also what makes Christianity compelling among the world's religions. And it is what can make your life compelling as well. Our crisis lies in the fact that we do not always believe that Jesus and the Holy Spirit are fully God alongside the Father.

This is a cosmic catastrophe that you might not care about, but here's why you should care: If you want to find value in your work, love in your relationships, and meaning in your faith, then it matters what you think about the Trinity. Only the Trinity reveals what it looks like to live selflessly and only the Trinity reveals how to be enlivened as our fullest selves. The life of God extended to us is our only source of peace, joy, significance, and belonging. It is this life that is our eternal life. It matters more than any book can really tell.

| LIVE LIKE IT MATTERS |

The end of every chapter has a short application under this heading. Don't skip them! Some of these applications you will resonate with or be challenged by, while others may not be your cup of tea. Each is one short thought or practical suggestion. I hope you will add your own thoughts and challenges as you read. Write down how what you are reading matters, and of course, act on it!

PART I

WHO MATTERS

2 WHOM WE'RE TALKING ABOUT

The Trinity is simply this: The three divine persons of Father, Son, and Holy Spirit, who are the one being of God. So the Trinity is three persons, one being—or one being, three persons. Each is fully Lord and fully God, yet there is only one Lord and one God. You see the three does not precede or create the one any more than the one precedes or creates the three. Neither is the unity of the three a fourth thing — the three is the one and the one is the three. It's the very definition of a paradox.

Whenever you see a pastor or theologian putting the one above the three or the three above the one (which is all the time), then he or she might be someone not quite comfortable with the paradoxical Trinity. It matters exactly what we mean by *person* and *being*, and more books than most of us could ever read have been written on the subject. Yet what Christians throughout history agree on is that God is tri-personal, yet the three participate in each other and dwell in each other so completely and perfectly that instead of having three minds, wills, and/or essences, they have only one. Each is himself fully God and a unique person, yet in and through each one we always find the other two. They are always one in being and one in action, yet in their relations to each other and to the world, they are three. Their unified work can be seen in Scripture from the initial act of creation through the final act of restoration at the end of time.

There is nothing exactly like it in our experience, and this makes sense, for God's creation is not the same thing as Godself. Perfect love, inasmuch as we can attain it, is perhaps the closest thing. *For us, the Trinity is at root always paradoxical and mysterious. Importantly, however, this does not make the Trinity unknowable.* Through God's revelation we know that God *is* personal, self-sacrificing love, and that the human image of this invisible God *is* Jesus.

It is true that in the Gospels we see that Jesus lowers himself and submits completely to the Father. Yet we miss the larger meaning and direction of Scripture when we use the texts describing Jesus' earthly ministry to overrule the texts that teach the eternal co-equality of the Trinitarian persons. Sadly, we do this all the time, causing us to miss the beauty of Christ's submission. God's willing sacrifice in Christ is twisted to become a command by God that a demi-god named Jesus merely follows. God as love makes us uncomfortable, because it implies that we should love, even when being crucified.

The average Christian can faithfully follow Jesus without wading into the waters of theology, but for many of us the time to dive in has come. The Trinity is a mystery, but our beliefs about it should not be. If we start with Jesus as the ultimate revelation given us, then we can let him define the Trinity for us. Three assumptions throughout this book are that Jesus is our foundation for understanding the Trinity, that the Trinity matters more than anything else, and that how we think about the Trinity is vital.

My first assumption is that Jesus is our foundation for everything. Christians don't dispute this, we just happen to have a habit of not living as if it were true! My bias is that Jesus is at the center of *all* things—of time, humanity, Scripture, and even eternity itself. Not because Jesus is greater than the Father or the Holy Spirit, but because Jesus is for us the way, the truth, and the life. We have no better "image of the invisible God" (Col. 1:15) and no other "exact representation of God's being" (Heb. 1:3 NIV). If we have seen the Father, it is because we have seen him through the Son, and if we have received the Holy Spirit, it is through the faith of, and our faith in, the Son. There is simply no better place to find God than in Jesus. In Jesus, we are invited into the life of the triune God who exists as an eternal act of perfect love.

In Jesus we see clearly not only what God looks like, but also what true humanity looks like. Since Jesus is fully human, sin, separation, and death no longer define human nature for those who are in Christ. Jesus is indeed more human than we are, opening the way for us to live into our own human fullness. In choosing the Tree of the Knowledge of Good and Evil, Adam and Eve chose their own way, their own solo dance that they thought would bring life but only brought death. They represent all of humanity, which has broken off from communion with God. The Good News is that the Trinity continues to extend divine life to us. Jesus did for us what we could not do for ourselves. He became one of us, defeated our sin and shame on the cross, and lived into the Trinitarian communion on our behalf.

My second assumption is that the Trinity matters more than anything else. I do agree that placing our faith in Jesus and loving God and each other is practically more important than understanding the Trinity. Following Jesus is the best way to come to understand who God is as the self-sacrificing, communal God of love. However, without the Trinity Christianity is no different from Islam, Judaism, atheism, pantheism, and—well, the list goes on. Many of these religious world views think highly of Jesus and the Spirit, but in their rejection of Son and Spirit as God, they have little room for a God who is Trinity. Sadly some Christians are tempted to think likewise, *yet without the Trinity, Christianity is pointless, and literally godless, for the Son and Spirit we have received turn out to not be God.*

My third assumption is that how we think about the Trinity is vital. There are raging theological questions that I will weigh in on without re-litigating each debate. If you don't understand some of the questions, don't worry too much, nobody really does. And of course, those who say they do have trouble agreeing. Yet the questions matter when it comes to answering the question that we really need to know: *How are we to live in light of the Trinity? Why does it matter?*

As an Anabaptist I come from a tradition in which belief must go beyond mental assent. True faith implies putting my trust in it and acting accordingly. If discipleship to Jesus is Trinitarian, then it should be reflected not just in Christian worship but in Christian behavior as well. Yet what exactly this behavior entails can be elusive, for while the Church is sometimes clear on the importance of the Trinity, our churches are often confused or just plain wrong on what it means. It is no wonder that most people think the doctrine of the Trinity is irrelevant.

To imagine how our thoughts of God actually are relevant, we will look at some models of the Trinity. I will illustrate an egalitarian model that incorporates the Scripture's portrayal of the Trinity's mutual submission and dependence. It will also integrate the contradictory eternal/temporal "trinities" as well as the conflicting Eastern/Western notions of the Trinity that are the source of many divisions. You can think of it as a "Trinitarian theory of everything," allowing the Trinity to better inform our faith, work, and life. The chapters are short, and between theological chapters will be lighter and more practical chapters. In these chapters I will offer some thoughts on how the Trinity can inform—and indeed transform—us in faith, work, and love. To paraphrase my wife; if our theology doesn't affect the lives of everyday people, then it isn't worth doing.

This book is for the pastors, teachers, and servant leaders of the Church. Should we accept the invitation, our God who is self-giving love has the power to transform our churches, our communities, and our lives. I hope a fresh understanding of the radical Jesus, the egalitarian Trinity, and the relational cosmos inspires you to love as God loves and to lead others in the way of Jesus Christ. The Trinity has eternal ramifications all the way up, and all the way down, and every which way you can imagine. Fear not, for a simple faith in Jesus is our guide and our destination as we work through matters of the Trinity.

| LIVE LIKE IT MATTERS |

In John 14:8-10, Philip asks Jesus to show the Father to him and the disciples:

Jesus said to him, "Have I been with you all this time, Philip, and you still do not know me? Whoever has seen me has seen the Father. How can you say, 'Show us the Father'? Do you not believe that I am in the Father and the Father is in me?"

Jesus is the perfect picture of who the Father is. Do you have a conception of God the Father that is characteristically different from Jesus? More angry or distant perhaps? Spend some time prayerfully aligning your picture of God with the one revealed by Jesus. Remember, Jesus reveals the character of the Father exactly!

3 WHEN IT COMES TO WORK, IT'S ABOUT THE WHO

Not the rock band. How the Trinity matters in our vocation.*

In my short lifetime I've worked in so many professions that I am practically unemployable: I have been a barista, health inspector, newspaper deliverer, cell culture biologist, theologian, stay-at-home dad, cashier, painter, regulatory manager, teacher, construction laborer, restaurant dishwasher, microbiologist, pharmaceutical manufacturer, produce clerk, real estate agent, and even a pastor and writer. Why so many different lines of work? There are a lot of reasons, most of which were not my choosing.

I've moved four times to help my wife follow her calling of being a pastor. With each move to seminary or to a new church posting, I've given up whatever profession I was in, moving on to a city or town where it was not possible to pursue my old profession. I also have very broad skills and interests, being the type who enjoys trying something new. Sometimes I try something and fail or learn that it is not for me, or I try something and the culture is too toxic to stay if I have any other choice.

More important than why I've landed in so many lines of work is what I've learned from them. In each I learned unique skills and perspectives. In each I worked with and grew to love and respect a different group of people. Some jobs were white-collar, others blue, and few no collar at all. In some I interacted with large numbers of customers, clients, and co-workers, while other jobs were more solitary. Each context had its own worldview as well as its unique conflicts and clashes of personalities. These jobs were spread out over thousands of miles in five states, and I've gained from the varied perspectives.

There is one thing I take away as a central piece of well-earned self-knowledge. The level of enjoyment and the amount of reward that I find in the job has less to do with the job itself and more to do with those I am working with, and who I am becoming. Yes, I've

---

* Nor the World Health Organization

worked in some bad environments with good people and not enjoyed it. Yet the culture only sets the stage; it lays the foundation for what is possible and whether growth and health is more or less likely. More important than the culture are the people, who experience and co-create the culture. It comes down to the "who." I will gladly do the worst of jobs, at least for a season, if I'm working with and for people who love and respect me, who labor alongside me, and who grow into true friends. Give me the best of jobs, and I will instantly become sour, unhappy, stressed out, and resentful if I'm working with and for people who do not love and respect me, who take advantage of me, who simply use me for their own ends, who, who, who . . . .

I've found that most people feel similarly when I talk to them about it. Whenever something close to reciprocal love enters your life, even just the superficial kind in professional environments, the heart finds a little bit of home. Most people don't leave bad jobs—they leave bad teams and bad bosses, and they stay for good ones. Of course anyone can work with the best team and still find themselves in a bad fit or role, feel called to something new, or experience any of a hundred reasons to move on. My purpose here is not to give career advice but simply to make this point—*as in work and life, when it comes to God it is all about the who. Show me your friends, family, and coworkers, and I will have a good sense of the kind of person you are becoming.*

My work journey has taught me something profound. What matters is not so much the "what" of your life, but who is in your life, and whose life you are in. With "who," it's not about quantity of people. It's not about finding perfect people. And it's not about going deep right away or feigning intimacy. It's about being free to be your genuine self while at the same time having people in your life who call you to be an even better self, more of your true self as God's unique image in the world. Life is about relationships in which we can express love, and true love always requires persons in relationship. And this is infinitely more true with God. The Trinity shows us that God *is* relational love—love that is mutual, reciprocal, and poured out freely on behalf of others.

This is why exactly where I work or exactly what I do is not my ultimate concern. My work does matter greatly to me, to the world, and to God, and your work matters greatly, so please don't mishear my point. It is as Paul says in his letter to the Corinthians: "If I give all I possess to the poor and give over my body to hardship that I may boast, but do not have love, I gain nothing."[1] Our work, like everything in life, matters only if it is done in love. We will find true belonging in any community only if we both give and receive love. And this love we find in community ultimately comes from God, who is love. Love is always relational. It is always about the person in front of us. It's about the "who," no matter the "what." The "what" matters only insofar as it helps us to love other persons, and be loved in return. So what matters in my work is not so much profession or place. What matters is that I find a little bit of the actual Trinity at work in my work life. It is then that my heart sings with joy.

| LIVE LIKE IT MATTERS |

The life giving work that God has for you to do can be anything, paid or unpaid, at home or away. It can be your day job, or not. If you haven't found your calling, it is time to engage relationally and pay attention to what brings you joy and connection. Take some personality profiles—whom has God made you to be? What bothers you and what are you passionate about fixing? Are you chasing after wealth or are you searching for God in the midst of your work? Remember, God is everywhere, but we all need a calling in which we find him, and in which the world finds him through us.

---

[1] 1 Corinthians 13:3 (NIV)

4 GODLESS CHRISTIANITY

We are uncomfortable with the paradoxes revealed by Jesus and prefer a watered down Trinity. Three is a crowd I guess.

I've heard it said that some things are "caught more than taught." The Trinity is one of those things in need of catching. That is not to say that churches don't teach about the Trinity, but what is taught and what is caught tend to be two different things. Growing up, I was taught that God is the Trinity, a paradox of three persons in one being; yet what I caught was that God is really a lone person, the Father.

We can teach one thing, but our words and deeds can demonstrate another. This is seen every day in comments within our churches, such as "I usually pray to God, but sometimes I pray to Jesus or the Holy Spirit," or "Jesus loves me, but I have trouble knowing that God does," or "We have the Spirit, but I wonder if God is present." Our language betrays our ambivalence about whether the Son and Spirit are God. We are conflicted—is the Trinity God in which Father, Son, and Spirit are each fully and equally God, or is the Father really God? In short, do we believe in the Trinity as God—in both a taught and a caught kind of way?

If we do not, then we may as well give up on the whole Christianity thing. The other religions have everything else our faith does, and they are less paradoxical. Just ask them—they think that Jesus and the Spirit are great and godly. Their main objection is that we believe that they are God! It is this very belief that makes belief in Jesus and Christianity itself good news. With the Trinity we have something powerful on our hands, if only we could catch it!

After conversations with hundreds of Christians across geography, age, and denomination, and after years studying the Trinity, I see that most Christians have an understanding that is not truly Trinitarian. This quasi-Trinitarianism goes by many labels such as "weak," "subordinationist," "gnostic," or "Arian" views of the Trinity. While the labels differ, they usually amount to the same thing: God is really the person of the Father over and above the

Trinity. With weak perceptions of the Trinity, we may think of the Son and Spirit as God in a taught kind of way, but if we don't perceive them as fully God, then we don't believe in the Trinity in a caught kind of way. Our belief will make no difference in our lives.

With weak Trinitarianism of the classical variety, God is a timeless Father who is God alone. This makes relationship with God impossible. God is powerless and presence-less in that Jesus and the Spirit are not fully God, making salvation and transformation impossible. Here we live as if God does not dwell among us in any real way in Son and Spirit, and the Father is too distant and un-relatable in his eternity to practically matter. *When we don't see Jesus as fully God, we are not likely to follow his teaching and example, and when we don't see the Spirit within us as fully God, we are not likely to believe that we can be transformed into people like Jesus.*

Yet with weak Trinitarianism of the modern, or New Age, variety, we can easily conflate God and the world and lose the God of Christianity. Here God is thought to be intimate and powerful, but is not distinguishable from human history or humanity generally. Being indistinguishable from us, this God cannot save us or enter into real relationship with us. This robs the Gospel of its power by taking from Christianity its divine essence. Take the Trinity away, and you don't have Christianity anymore. Or at least, Christianity doesn't have God anymore.

At the heart of Christianity are two indivisible paradoxes revealed in the person, ministry, and teaching of Jesus: the Trinity and the dual nature of Jesus. These paradoxes each seem self-contradictory in and of themselves as matters of faith, yet a deeper logical problem is that the two paradoxes seem to contradict not just themselves, but also each other! If we accept that the one God exists as three persons who are each fully God, then how can one of those persons be fully human? God obviously isn't human, right? God is God! How can Jesus be one with God and also be united with humanity? In the minds of many, something has to give, and what invariably gives is both the Trinity and the dual nature of Jesus, because the two are joined in Jesus Christ, the crux of Christianity. You can't have the

Jesus of Scripture without these paradoxes, but oh, how we avoid them!

While many of us would never say that Jesus *is not* God, we often don't fully believe that Jesus *really is* God. The same often goes for his humanity. Sadly, this makes the Trinity God in name only, and it makes the doctrine irrelevant. Changing this situation requires an embrace of paradox rather than the customary retreat from it. The paradox of three persons in one being should be joined by the paradox of Jesus being fully human and fully God. We traditionally have kept these paradoxes separate, and for good reasons, but *it's better to let the paradoxes define each other, for they are intrinsically linked in the person of Jesus.*

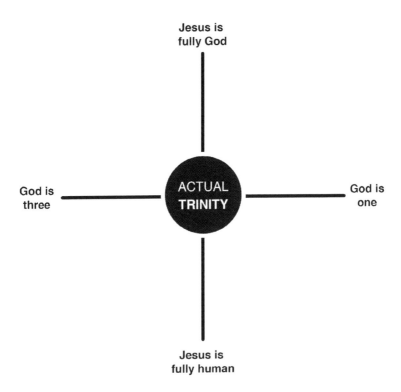

Figure 1: The Double Paradox

If we plot them together we get this picture, which we will add to a little later. And we will look at other models and illustrations. First, however, we need to lay a Trinitarian foundation. The Trinity has neither made much sense nor been practical because we resist taking it to its radical and logical conclusion, where each divine person is fully and equally God *and* where Jesus is simultaneously fully human. You see, all the claims we make to our children about who Jesus is and how God saves us make sense only with the Trinity, for it is the mark of Christianity. It is who God is, existing as a community of eternal love that we are invited into. Only through the Trinity are we created, redeemed, and restored, and only in the Trinity are we oriented Godward. There is no Gospel outside it. Without it, the Good News comes to an impasse, with the road to salvation closed. Apart from the Trinity we are left with a Godless Christianity. Thankfully, this is not the Gospel of Jesus Christ!

| LIVE LIKE IT MATTERS |

As Christians, what marks us out theologically is the Trinity. Jesus and the Spirit are not just good, and they are not just from God; they are God. Yet what distinguishes us practically should be our love. God as Trinity is love. Our love for ourselves and others comes from God. And Jesus says that everyone will know we are his followers by our love for one another.[2] The love of God is not a feeling, though feelings can accompany it. The love of God is sacrificial action on behalf of another, and it never makes God any less.

This is what we should celebrate and sing songs about. So when you next sing songs of praise to God which talk about God's sacrificial love, think more about action and sacrifice and less about cultural notions of romance. And since Jesus is God, we should act like it and obey his commands! These are summed up by loving as God loves us.

---

[2] John 13:35

21

5 AND WE DANCE

Waltz? Tango? No. Perichoresis—the life of God in motion.

Whether you call it a word, analogy, or a doctrine, *perichoresis* has become the standard idea in theology to envision the God of Scripture revealed as Father, Son, and Holy Spirit. Perichoresis refers to the mutual inter-animation of the three divine persons who perfectly indwell each other, constituting God's unified being. It seems to derive from the Greek roots *peri* (around) and *chorein* (to give away). The latter is also the origin of the English word *choreography*. Perichoresis is the divine dance of self-giving love that is the triune God. In this dance, each member pours himself out into the others, even as he is filled by the others. They inter-animate and interpenetrate each other so completely that they are one perfect essence—one mind, will, and being. The term was used by the Church Fathers in combating Arianism in the fourth century; John of Damascus formalized it as a doctrine in the eighth century.

This perichoretic dance is an eternal movement in which Father, Son, and Spirit submit in love to each other, even as each is empowered by each other. In their one perfect being, the three are each their unique selves as they surrender to and enliven each other. While this is an eternal movement outside of creation, the only reason we know about it is because we have seen it characterized within creation. It overflows to us in the acts of creating, redeeming, and sanctifying the world. Scripture reveals to us that the work of the Trinity in the world is the same eternal dance of the Trinity beyond time—in all eternity.

Imagine it with me.

ETERNITY

Imagine a God who exists eternally as a community of three equally divine persons. The relational communion of the three is so perfect that they are one divine being. And this one relational God is love. This love is dynamic—open to the other, to giving and receiving. Each divine person exists in and through this love. Each pours himself out sacrificially on behalf of the other two, even as he is filled by the other two. The one constitutes the three, while the three constitutes the one. This is the eternal dance of love.

CREATION

Now imagine that God chooses to extend this love beyond Godself, to overflow it into something new. So God creates the universe. In an act of self-limitation and sacrifice, God pulls back to make room for something other than God. The Spirit takes the lead in the eternal dance and hovers over the primordial "waters" of this void. The Spirit then pours himself out into the Father and the Son, overflowing the eternal dance of love into creation. Through his self-emptying, the Spirit sends the Father as Creator and gives divine power over our creation to the Son, through whom all things are created. And it was good.

Then God said, "Let *us* make humankind in *our* image, according to *our* likeness."[3] Male and female, individuals created in the image of the one God, yet together created in the image of the communal God who exists through interpersonal relationships. And it was very good. Yet there were bound to be problems for a Creator who is love, for love requires persons who are free to accept or to reject their part in the dance, persons who are free to choose for or against relationship. And so the relational barrier of sin and death infects and separates humanity from God. Yet from eternity the Trinity had chosen a solution to our problem. A solution with a great cost.

REDEMPTION

Imagine that the Father takes the lead in the eternal dance. Reciprocating the work of the Spirit, he pours himself out into the Son and Spirit, the dance of love overflowing. In self-emptying, the Father sends the Son as Redeemer and gives divine power over our redemption to the Spirit. The Son temporarily gives up his divine privileges and becomes fully human. God submits to becoming a part

---

[3] Genesis 1:26 (italics mine).

of creation, yet God cannot stop being God. He takes on our fallen humanity—a humanity that can sin like us—but through obedience to the Father and submission to the Spirit, Jesus does not sin like us, making a way for us. In Jesus, God is perfectly represented for us, and the character of God is fully seen in his submitted, self-giving, Spirit-empowered life.

God makes space within eternity for humanity, for God and humanity exist perfectly and paradoxically together in the person of Jesus Christ. Now watch how sin and its curse—our suffering, alienation, even death itself—is taken upon Jesus on the cross, causing him to experience a loss of communion with the Father and the Spirit. He feels abandoned. "Why have you forsaken me!" he cries, echoing the lament of Psalm 22. Yet Jesus does not reject his humanity—he knows the Psalm ends in the good and perfect peace between God and us. The Spirit empowers him to be faithful to the end.

God pours Godself out for us, and takes the consequences of sin and death upon himself. As Jesus speaks his last words, he commends his Spirit into the arms of God. And then he takes his last, dying breath. The dance seems to end abruptly. It is hard to imagine. Yet the Father and Spirit do not let go of their beloved, for the being of God cannot be broken. What is the Trinity to do when Jesus dies? What they always do, and had purposed to do all along— they dance. God makes space for humanity as Jesus extends the dance straight through sin, suffering, and death.

Jesus never lets humanity go, and Father and Spirit never let Jesus go. Jesus is one with us and one with Father and Spirit. Thus God holds onto us through death itself. The Trinity reaches through the very core of darkness, and there Jesus falls in complete trust into the embrace of Father of and Spirit. And the Trinity dances, this time on both sides of the relational barrier, and this dance shatters sin and death, raising Jesus from the dead. And so begins the good and perfect peace of a new creation.

SANCTIFICATION

Imagine now that the risen Son reciprocates, taking the lead in the eternal dance. All authority in heaven and earth has been given to him, so he pours himself out into the Spirit and the Father, the dance of love overflowing. In doing so he sends the Spirit as our Restorer, who is actively preparing the world for Jesus' return. Jesus waits for the time when all things will be reconciled to God, when he will give all things back to the Father. And the Father, who knows the day of final restoration, works, and waits, and loves.

The powers of evil and death have suffered a mortal blow. We can live through our own suffering and death knowing that like Christ's, it will end in total victory and reunion with our beloved God. Soon the day will come when time and space will be folded into eternity. For those who say yes to God, the dance draws us in. For in Jesus—who holds both divine and human, eternal and temporal, heaven and earth, perfectly and paradoxically together—the dance has been extended to you and to me. Jesus reaches out his hand and asks you to follow him, desiring you to join this eternal movement of love, or what he simply calls "eternal life."

| LIVE LIKE IT MATTERS |

When two dancers perform in perfect partnership, it becomes one dance, not two. Two become one. With the Trinity it is profoundly more so. The three do not become one, *they are one*. In Jesus, God has made room for us to join the dance, but we are not very good at following God's lead. Both partners can't lead at the same time. Dancing requires simultaneous initiative and surrender. It requires leading and following, compromise and improvisation. And above all, it requires practice. So does life. Marriage is one way to practice. Friendships are another. Who is your dance partner right now? How are you called to initiate and lead? How are you called to surrender? How can you improvise together? If dancing is like the life of God, then our life reflects that creativity. Show up and practice today. In time, you'll catch the rhythm.

6 HOW JESUS VIEWS HIMSELF

The Trinity is our understanding because it is Jesus' self-understanding.

You might wonder why I would say that faith in the Trinity is the mark of Christianity; what about faith in Jesus Christ? Actually, Jesus and the Trinity are inseparable. It is Jesus who defines Christianity for us. While he is fully human and able to perfectly identify with us, he is simultaneously perfectly one being with the Father and the Holy Spirit. It is only in the Trinity that we correctly envision who Jesus is.

When we look at the New Testament, we find that Jesus not only acknowledges his obvious humanity, but he also teaches that he is fully God. And he is not only God, but he also understands himself through his relationship with the Father and the Holy Spirit. In other words—brace yourself—the Trinity is not only how we ought to understand God, but it is how God understands Godself! Jesus gives us this crazy idea. He made a lot of powerful enemies by equating himself with God. Sometimes he did so with direct statements to the effect of "I am God." Here is an example from John chapter 8: "Jesus said to them, 'Very truly I tell you, before Abraham was, I AM.' So they picked up stones to throw at him, but Jesus hid himself and went out of the temple."[4]

Jesus calls himself *I AM*, a direct reference the burning bush when Moses asked after the name of the God he was encountering. God answered Moses, "I AM WHO I AM," and then created a relational context by saying, "the God of your fathers—the God of Abraham, the God of Isaac, and the God of Jacob. . . . This is my name forever and ever."[5] Jesus' audience clearly understood that he was equating himself with God's very being, hence the stone throwing. Not only did Jesus boldly name himself God, he also boldly did things that only God had the authority to do: [When he saw their faith he said, "Friend, your sins are forgiven you." Then the scribes and the Pharisees began to question, "Who is this who is

---

[4] John 8:58
[5] Exodus 3:14–15 (NIV)

speaking blasphemies? Who can forgive sins but God alone?"[6]] Jesus said that to welcome him was to welcome God,[7] and that to have seen him was to have seen God.[8] Even when faced with violence, Jesus continued to insist on his identity as God.

> The Jews took up stones again to stone him. Jesus replied, "I have shown you many good works from the Father. For which of these are you going to stone me?" The Jews answered, "It is not for a good work that we are going to stone you, but for blasphemy, because you, though only a human being, are making yourself God."[9]

It is true that some biblical passages are ambiguous regarding the full divinity of Jesus, while many simply focus on his humanity; yet others, such as the following from John's Gospel, are as clear as possible: "In the beginning was the Word, and the Word was with God, and the Word was God."[10] The passage goes on to say that "no one has ever seen God, but the one and only Son, who is himself God, and is in closest relationship with the Father, has made him known."[11] Paul also made the case when admonishing the church in Philippi to be like Jesus in their relationships with each other. Likely writing before any of the Gospels had been penned, he quotes a hymn recited by the very first generation of Christians:

"In your relationships with one another, have the same mindset as Christ Jesus:

> *Who, being in very nature God,*
> *did not consider equality with God*
> *as something to be used to his own advantage;*
> *rather, he made himself nothing*
> *by taking the very nature of a servant,*
> *being made in human likeness.*

---

[6] Luke 5:20-21
[7] Matthew 10:40, Mark 9:37
[8] John 14:9
[9] John 10:31–33
[10] John 1:1
[11] John 1:18 (NIV)

And being found in appearance as a man,
he humbled himself
by becoming obedient to death—
even death on a cross!"[12]

Jesus is fully God, both ontologically—in his being, and functionally—in his action. As Paul said, he is in very nature God and fully equal to God, yet gave up divine privileges to become fully human. When Jesus described himself with phrases like "the Father and I are one,"[13] the response from the people is that they *again* pick up stones to kill him, for they know he is claiming to be God—a great blasphemy for his Jewish audience. Jesus demonstrates that God is ultimately relational. Jesus' self-understanding is his relationship, indeed his relational unity, with the Father and the Holy Spirit. In the Gospels we find this powerful notion: *It is in the relational Trinity that Jesus understands and reveals who he is.*

So who or what is the Trinity? Again we look to Jesus: "Go therefore and make disciples of all nations, baptizing them in the name of the Father, and of the Son, and of the Holy Spirit."[14] In the Great Commission, Jesus puts together for us what is previously in the Gospels only implied: The transcendent I AM who is beyond adequate naming, the same relational God of Abraham, Isaac, and Jacob, is revealed to us as the three persons of Father, Son, and Holy Spirit. And the Greek text of the Great Commission makes clear that the three divine persons share a *single* name, a name that Jesus doesn't quite give. Together the Father, Son, and Spirit share the reality we know as God. GOD IS WHO GOD IS, and God has been revealed to us as Father, Son, and Holy Spirit. This understanding of God is the Christian understanding, precisely because it is Christ's understanding.

So is God one or three? Clearly, the three divine persons are somehow distinct. When Jesus is talking to the Father, he is not

---

[12] Philippians 2:5–8 (NIV)
[13] John 10:30
[14] Matthew 28:19, emphasis added.

merely talking to himself. The Father, Son, and Spirit are each unique persons. The Spirit was not nailed to a cross, nor was the Father resurrected on Easter Sunday. Jesus would not have bothered to describe his relationship with Father and the Spirit if they were just three expressions of one divine person. That is the heresy of modalism, the belief that God is three modes, or manifestations of a single divine person. We have one God, but we have three persons constituting this one being of love. Love requires a community of self-giving persons.

The Bible is clear that each divine person is distinct from the others, yet Jesus repeatedly talks about their oneness: "May they be one as we are one."[15] The Gospels portray the Father, Son, and Holy Spirit as a relational God characterized by perfect unity.[16] The Scriptures never reference more than one true God. This leaves tritheism, the heresy that says there are three gods, lacking in any scriptural foundation. If we are to take the biblical witness seriously, then we are left with the profound paradox that God is three *and* God is one. God is Trinity. This understanding, following the logic inherent in the Gospels, was eventually clarified by the Church to say that *God is triune in that God is "three persons, one being."*

In response to the experience of the incarnation of Jesus Christ and the indwelling of the Holy Spirit, the faith of the early Christians was a Trinitarian faith. They went to the ends of the world, baptizing in the name of the Father, the Son, and the Holy Spirit. And they proclaimed a Trinitarian Gospel of salvation that was far more powerful and profound than the misguided and not so Trinitarian alternative—with a prophet or demigod named Jesus and a supernatural force called the Holy Spirit.

The early Christians perceived that God extends salvation to humankind precisely because Jesus and the Holy Spirit *are* God. The first Christians were devout Jews, and they generally reserved the title "Lord" for Yahweh alone. "Hear, O Israel: The Lord is our God, the

---

[15] John 17: 11, 21, 22

[16] The Gospel of John, chapters 14–17 is an example in which the Trinitarian relationship is characterized simultaneously by unity and dynamism.

Lord alone."[17] The Shema, as it is called, is still foundational for Judaism today. Calling Jesus and the Holy Spirit "Lord" was to say that Jesus and the Spirit are the one true God of Israel. And this is exactly what they did.

There is in Christianity no demi-God, quasi-God, or semi-God in addition to God. There is either God or not God. *Indeed, if Jesus and the Spirit are anything less than fully God, then God was never among us in the person of Jesus, nor is God with us now in the person of the Holy Spirit.* It is God alone, not one of God's creatures or extensions, who creates, redeems, and sanctifies us. If Jesus and the Spirit are anything less than fully God, then the salvation of humankind does not depend on the person of Jesus, and Christianity is indeed a lie.

In Jesus God has chosen to identify with us in a profound way. The sinless humanity of Jesus becomes essential to who God is for us, chosen from all eternity. Through Jesus we are invited to "participate in the divine nature" as 2 Peter 1:4 describes—the relationship among the Father, Son, and Spirit. It is this relationship that created the world, is redeeming the world, and will bring the world and heaven back together at the End. It is more powerful than death. It is even now working to restore us to God and to each other. This is Good News! If we believed it, and if we could live into this perfect love it could transform the world. Yet for all of our talk, works of art, and doctrine about the Trinity, do we really believe that three persons are completely, fully, and equally one God? Would you bet your life on the Trinity, as Jesus did on the cross?

---

[17] Deuteronomy 6:4

| LIVE LIKE IT MATTERS |

That the Son and Spirit are just as divine as the Father does not mean that they boss each other around. They don't have three competing wills as three of us would have—they have one perfectly unified will. Our churches and communities should reflect that. We should not be lording over each other, and we should be of one mind and one will when it comes to the Church's mission in the world.

What is the unified will of the church you attend? Most of us probably do not know because many churches do not articulate a clear and *specific* mission, vision, and values. We avoid such specifics to avoid bickering, but more disagreement results over the long term. We will not agree on what our priorities should be without a unified mission and a strategy to implement it. We will never see eye to eye without having a specific vision of where our particular community is going. And we will never agree on how to get there without having common values. This applies more to pastors, elders and board members, but please, let's be of one mind as God expects. We can start as leaders by being specific, by listening to the stories and values of those in our community, and by repeatedly communicating where we are going.

7 PARENTING AND PERICHORESIS

Parenting is proof that being God is hard work.

A picture I see in my family, and in families generally, reflects the Trinity. My wife and I pour out our lives for our daughter so that she may have life. In doing so, we often experience new life and tremendous joy as well, but the relationship is asymmetrical. Physically, financially, emotionally—our lives are now being drained even as Imogen's is being filled. We take care of ourselves as best we can, yet even doing that is now largely in the service of her long-term interests and not merely our own. We still have dreams and aspirations, but we are increasingly aware of our own mortality. We gave life, and soon our own will slowly drain away. We are all temporal, time-bound, temporary. We are dust, and to dust we will return.

It is the same with my own parents. They emptied themselves so that my brother and sisters and I could be filled. They did so imperfectly, and sometimes with the wrong motives, just as Meredith and I do so imperfectly now with our daughter. Many parents have children out of selfish motives, but if they end up being even half-decent parents, they too will pour out on behalf of their children. The lives of my parents continue through my own life, and then through Imogen's, but soon a day will come when no one remembers who any of us were. Our active part in creation will have come to an end.

Or will it? The life of the Trinity would suggest otherwise. Family is one of the primary analogies used to describe aspects of the Trinitarian relationship. The three persons of the Trinity exist as an act of perfect communion, continually emptying into each other even as they are continually being filled by each other. Their very identity is found in their uniting relationship. It is a picture of divine mutuality and reciprocity that human families can reflect. Our parents pour into us, and hopefully we grow and thrive. If our parents are lucky, we will someday pour back into them before their lives draw to a close, even as we pour into any children of our own.

The Gospel invites the entire human community—the one family of God—to experience God's love through submission and service to each other. The Trinity lives out this love reciprocally, perfectly, dynamically, and eternally. It is literally what life is all about. Each person of the Trinity exists through this dance of communion that is the source of all life. We experience it in creation, redemption, and restoration, and we participate in this communion ourselves through our loving relationships. Parents reflect the self-emptying dynamic in the raising of their children. They give of themselves in order to fill others, who in turn will grow up to pour themselves out and bring life to the world in unique ways.

In giving and receiving love from each other we catch a glimpse of who God is. Since we are made in the image of God, mutual empowerment in mutual submission is what characterizes human community at its best. But we are also fallen. We are unwilling to submit because there are those who would take advantage of us. We fear to submit because our lives are short, and we are only human, after all. It is one thing to be God and submit to God, and quite another to be human and submit to my spouse, my parent, and my neighbor. Never mind my enemy. We are human, and the persons of the Trinity are not human as we are, and they do not die as we do. *Except Jesus is, and Jesus did.*

The God who gives life is a God of sacrifice. Jesus invites us to join God's family, but to take part we must join in the dance of sacrificial submission and empowerment. Jesus said it well: "You must lose your life in order to find it." It is a truth he knows as a person of the Trinity, for he trusted in it enough to put off his divine power and privilege and become one of us. In pouring himself out completely on the cross, the way is opened for us to die his death as well—a death that leads to life everlasting. To be a Christian means to believe against all evidence to the contrary that a life poured out for others, a life emptied on behalf the world, does not end in death, but in resurrection and eternal life. Pouring out one's life on behalf of another is to live in God's image, and it is a life worth celebrating.

| LIVE LIKE IT MATTERS |

Are you a parent? It can be the hardest thing you'll ever do, and it can make you feel pretty lousy about life at times. Remember that your primary ministry as a parent is your children. You are to be making them into disciples of Jesus. A disciple is *a learner*, and your job is not to shame children for misbehavior, but to help them learn from it. A parent's discipline, therefore, should be motivated by what children will learn, rather than simply making them feel pain or shame.

Shame is not the same as guilt. Guilt says *what I have done is not worthy of me*. Shame says that *I am unworthy and incapable of doing good*. Shame prevents us from learning anything other than that we aren't capable of doing any better. So let's be like Jesus and teach our kids to do better. Their actions may be unworthy of them, but they are not themselves unworthy of love—yours or Gods. People learn best in environments of love. Fear and shame will inhibit you from receiving love and from pouring out your life in love. And kids need love. Lord Jesus, help us to love our children as you love us.

8 HOW THE CHURCH CAME TO BELIEVE IN THE TRINITY

And explain the Arian texts supporting subordination of the Son.

It might be helpful at this point to do four things in order for us to work with the same foundation. First, I will define the Trinity. Second, I will reference some Bible verses that round out the doctrine of the Trinity. Third, I will give the simplest of historical overviews in regard to how the Church developed this belief. And last, I will give the historical Church's briefest explanation of the biblical texts that would seem to go against Trinitarianism in favor of God as the Father alone.

On to the first task. The Trinity is the three persons of Father, Son, and Holy Spirit who are one God.

- They have one divine being and one will.
- They are co-equal (equally God) and co-eternal (existing from all eternity).
- They exist in complete interpersonal dependence through sacrificial love. Each is fully God, and together they are fully God.
- They each take on specific work for the purposes of creation, redemption, and restoration of the world, yet one never acts apart from the others. They act as one.
- In these actions they freely submit to each other, but in their submission they are never less God in any way.

That is the Trinity in a nutshell. A major takeaway is that God is not synonymous with the Father alone. The Son and Spirit are also equally God and are one being with the Father. Since they are one in being, there is no "chain of being" descending from the Father. And since they are one in action, there is no "chain of command" descending from the Father.[18] Of course much more can be said about this topic, but let's move on to Scripture before looking at

---

[18] Kevin Giles, *The Trinity and Subordinationism: The Doctrine of God and the Contemporary Gender Debate* (Downers Grove, IL: InterVarsity Press, 2002), 1-105.

Church history.

The Bible does not contain the word "Trinity." That is no reason to give up on God as Trinity, for even the word "Bible" isn't in the Bible. So why do we insist on the Trinity when there is no explicit definition of it given to us within the pages of Scripture? Because the Bible doesn't make any sense or contain much value without it. The Trinity is clearly integral to Jesus' teaching as well as the New Testament as a whole. The first Christians, who were Jewish, would not have referred to Jesus as "Lord" lightly. To call anyone but God "Lord" was blasphemy. Yet Scripture even calls the Holy Spirit "Lord" twice in 2 Corinthians 3:17-18.

What follows are some key themes from Scripture that come together to form our Trinitarian understanding. I won't belabor the point by typing out every reference. These are given to you in bulleted form to look up on your own. While not every passage is clearly Trinitarian, when they are read in light of Christ the overall Trinitarian nature of Scripture becomes quite clear.

- **God is one**
  (Deuteronomy 6:4, 1 Corinthians 8:4, Galatians 3:20, 1 Timothy 2:5)

- **Yet God is three**
  Even in the Old Testament God sometimes speaks to God-self in the plural:
  "Let *us* make humankind in *our* image" (Genesis 1:26),[19] also (Genesis 3:22, 11:7, Isaiah 6:8, and examples from the Psalms)

- **The Father is God**
  (John 6:27, 1 Peter 1:2)

- **Jesus, while human, is also God**
  "Jesus said to them, 'Very truly I tell you, before Abraham was, I

---

[19] The plural Elohim in Genesis does not itself prove the Trinity, but when read theologically in light of Christ, which is how I read the entire Bible, the Trinity becomes apparent.

AM.'" (John 8:58)

Jesus said that to welcome him was to welcome God. (Matthew 10:40, Mark 9:37)

Jesus said that to have seen him was to have seen God. (John 14:9)

- **The Bible's explicit references to Jesus as God**
  "The Word was God." (John 1:1)
  "The one and only Son, who is himself God ..." (John 1:18)
  "Who being in very nature God, did not consider equality with God ..." (Philippians 2:5–8)
  "Jesus is God over all." (Romans 9:5)

- **Jesus is of one being and will with the Father**
  (John 10:30, 14-17)

- **Jesus is also one with the Spirit**
  (Acts 16:7, Galatians 4:6, Philippians 1:19, 1 Peter 1:11)

- **The Holy Spirit is God**
  The Spirit of God is the first mention in Scripture of any of the three divine persons. (Genesis 1:2)
  The Spirit is eternal. (Hebrews 9:14)
  The Lord is the Spirit. (2 Corinthians 3:17-18)
  "God is Spirit, and his worshippers must worship in the Spirit and in truth." (John 4:24)

- **The Spirit is a person, referred to by Jesus with personal pronouns.** (John 15:26, 16:12–15)

- **God is not three versions of one person, but three persons.** (John 14:16–17, etc.)

- **The Great Commission.**
  "Go therefore and make disciples of all nations, baptizing them in the *name of the Father, and the Son, and the Holy Spirit.*" (Matthew 28:19). The Greek implies that all three have one name.

This is just the tip of the iceberg, but it makes the point that Scripture witnesses to the Trinity in many ways. I will admit that it is not the most logical idea. The dual nature of the Son and the tri-unity of God are conjoined paradoxes. Some may find this disheartening, but for me all of the radical, impossible, and miraculous claims of Christianity begin to make perfect sense when the double paradox of Jesus is accepted as our starting point. Leading with paradox may not win you awards in logic class, but it will go a long way in being a disciple of Jesus. After all, "those who find their life will lose it, and those who lose their life for my sake will find it."[20]

Now on to the third task: How did we end up with the Trinity historically? The Israelites came from a polytheistic context, yet they were supposed to be monotheists. Of course they often lapsed into worshipping the gods of the nations around them, making them polytheists. Whether in practice the Israelites were monotheists or polytheists, it is fair to say that the Old Testament Hebrews did not believe in the Trinity as Christians do now.

With the advent of Jesus and the indwelling of the Spirit, the early Christians had to wrestle with their Jewish monotheism and their experience of God in three distinct persons. It would soon become clear that not everyone agreed on how best to think about it. Christians worshipped Father, Son, and Holy Spirit, but questions and disagreements existed around key points:

- What does it mean that each was God?
- Is the Father greater, as Jesus said, and if so, in what way?
- Did the Father create the Son and/or Spirit?
- How are they the one God of the Old Testament?

The word "Trinity" was adopted late in the second century and thereafter become widespread, yet views on what it meant varied, and use of the term did little to answer the above questions.

By the early fourth century, Arianism (named after Arius) was

---

[20] Matthew 10:39

gaining prominence. Arius and others taught that Jesus was a created being and therefore not fully God, even though he is like a god to us. Other church leaders reacted strongly against Arianism, which led to the First Ecumenical Council in Nicaea in the year 325. The council strongly affirmed the full divinity of Jesus and stated clearly that he is not a created being. From Nicaea we get the beginnings of the Nicene Creed. Yet as soon as this issue was settled (officially), the question moved on to that of the divinity of the Holy Spirit.

Five decades later, Macedonianism (named after Macedonius), was being argued. Macedonianism is the belief that the Holy Spirit is a created being—a type of Arianism applied to the Spirit. This helped lead to the Second Ecumenical Council in Constantinople in the year 381, which affirmed the full divinity and personhood of the Spirit. From Constantinople we received the completed Nicene Creed, sometimes called the Nicene-Constantinopolitan Creed. A core issue of the Trinity was still not resolved, however.

As soon as the full divinity of the Son and Spirit was settled, the question quickly moved on to how Jesus can be fully God yet be fully human at the same time. It seemed logically impossible to some that Jesus could be both fully human and fully God, and Nestorianism (named after Nestorius) argued that Jesus' humanity and divinity consisted of two separate human and divine persons. This led to the Third and Fourth Ecumenical Councils, in Ephesus in the year 431 and Chalcedon in 451. Here the Church affirmed that Jesus is not half human and half God, nor is he two separate human and divine persons, but he is inseparably one person who is both fully human and fully divine. So Jesus is one person with two inseparable, yet distinguishable natures.

On to the final task of this chapter. The Arians employed an impressive array of verses from the Bible to make their case that the Son was created and otherwise inferior to the Father. The great teachers of the Church at the time, such as Athanasius, and after him the Cappadocians and Augustine, argued that while individual texts could be used to prove anything, the overall thrust of Scripture was Trinitarian. No divine person was before or after, above or below, lesser or greater, than the others. The passages which spoke of the subordination of the Son were true, but limited to Jesus' earthly ministry. That is, they are to be understood as a temporary condition caused by Jesus giving up his divine privileges, taking on humanity and bearing the cross. They were not to be understood as a permanent or eternal state of the Son.

Off-the-mark teachings (traditionally called heresies) clearly played a role in the development of the doctrine of the Trinity over time by forcing the Church to answer previously unanswered questions. The philosophical categories of the day were assumed by both sides and were employed in their arguments. There was no need to state a doctrine of the Trinity until what was believed to be false teachings began gaining acceptance. The councils did not invent the belief, but the belief was made explicit in order to counter teaching that went against the scriptural witness and early Christian understanding.

| LIVE LIKE IT MATTERS |

Are you more comfortable with Jesus as human or Jesus as God? It's OK to lean more to one side or another at times. The problem is that we are accustomed to viewing him as in between human and God—the worst of both worlds.

How do you live like Jesus is God? You worship him, learn from him, and obey him. You spend time reading the Gospels, getting to know him.

How do you live like Jesus is human? You accept that the human portrayal of Jesus in the Gospels is the exact representation of God as a human being. And you live as he did—being open to the Holy Sprit and submitting to the Father in heaven, confident that you can live your life just as he did.

This is what faith in Jesus looks like, and it results in a resurrection unto eternal life!

9 WHO SHOULD I PRAY TO?

I am tired of saying whom.

Pastors get this question a lot: If God is three persons, to whom are we supposed to pray? The short answer is that we should only and always pray to God. Yet here it matters whether we conceive of God as the Father primarily, or as the communion of the three persons who are each fully God. If God is the Father alone in your view, then you do not believe in the Trinity, and you should for the sake of principle pray to the Father alone. If you believe that Father, Son and Spirit are one divine being, then you are free to pray to any of and all of the three persons, for each is fully God, and the communion of God will hear your prayers addressed to any or all.

The short answer above suffices, but there is a longer answer worth noting. Since Jesus is the person of the Trinity who is also human, he is our example to emulate. He taught us the Lord's Prayer in which the Father is addressed. Jesus prayed to the Father through the Holy Spirit, so we also are to pray in Jesus, to the Father in heaven, through the Holy Spirit who indwells us. The Lord's Prayer is striking in that it is the only example I'm aware of in Scripture where Jesus refers to the Father not as "my Father" or even "your Father" but as "*our* Father." Through the grace of God given in Jesus we come to share in the life of the Trinity. In joining with the faith of Jesus, his Father becomes our Father, his Spirit becomes our Spirit, and his full and perfect humanity becomes our humanity.

While Jesus is our model and teacher, we also need to remember that we are not Jesus. He is God and we are not. That Jesus lowered himself by becoming human did not make him any less God; it simply reveals the self-sacrificing character of God's love. Therefore, we are free to also pray to Jesus and the Holy Spirit. The Bible encourages us to have a relationship with them, and I'm not sure how else to go about that other than praying.

God is love, and God is not a vindictive monitor of our prayer formulas, waiting for us to get it wrong to then punish us accordingly. God is always pursuing communion with us, and God is of one mind. Praying to either Father, Son, or Spirit is praying to God, and we should pray to God, who is Father, Son, and Holy Spirit.

| LIVE LIKE IT MATTERS |

Who do you pray to? If you are in a prayer rut, try expanding your horizons a little. If you are someone who doesn't usually pray to Jesus or the Spirit, then now is the time to start. Right this moment is fine. Or perhaps you haven't thought of prayer as communing with all three persons at once. They are one being, mind, and will, so your prayers have always done this, but it helps if you know that this is happening. God as Spirit is in you, praying for you, even while God as Son is praying with you, even while God as Father is receiving your prayer. Prayer is as simple as talking to God, and as complicated as you could ever imagine!

So, pray! It doesn't have to look a certain way. Pray during exercise, at work, at parties. Pray your joys and your darkest moments. Open up your heart to God. He is in the world around you, in you, and far beyond you, all at once.

10 SIGHTING THE TRINITY

The double paradox of the Trinity and Jesus—illustrating who God is, and who God is not.

A key to understanding the Trinity is to behold the two paradoxes simultaneously revealed in Jesus Christ: God is both three and one, and Jesus is both human and God.

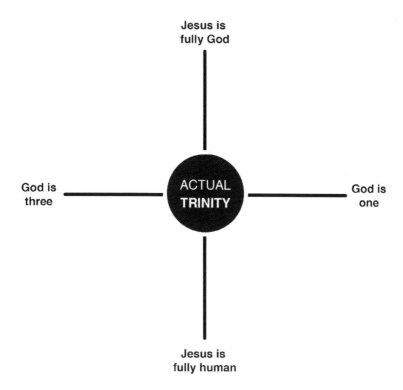

Figure 1: The Double Paradox

I've drawn them out to illustrate what it looks like to hold the tension of both paradoxes. G.K. Chesterton is often quoted as saying that "a paradox is truth standing on its head to attract attention." If that is true, then God is working doubly hard to get our attention! The diagram looks like a target or sights on a scope, and should be used in a similar way. *When we cross-link the paradoxes, being Jesus centered is defined by being Trinitarian centered, and being Trinitarian centered is defined by being Jesus centered.* When we are trying to sight the Trinity, we need to look through both paradoxes at the same time to find dead center. When we fail to hold the double tension at the center, we end up on an outer circle where we find 10 various positions we can land on when the center does not hold.

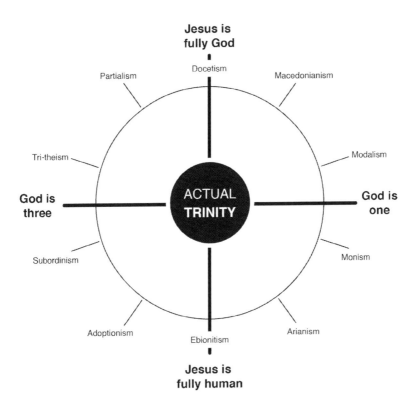

Figure 2: The Double Paradox With the Outer Rim

On the outer circle are 10 common misunderstandings (or heresies) one lands on when the proper tension is not held. Other heresies could fit here also, but these 10 well represent the full spectrum in my opinion. I call this circle of misunderstanding the "outer rim." Which side of a paradox you over-emphasize will determine where you land on the rim. Starting with Monism on the right and then moving around clockwise, here are the descriptions of each:

- **Monism** – There is no Trinity, just a single divine person who is God.
- **Arianism** – Jesus is more than human, yet he is created by the Father and less than fully God.
- **Ebionitism** – While special, Jesus is not divine; he is only human.
- **Adoptionism** – Jesus was born human and not divine, but was adopted by God and granted divinity by God.
- **Subordinationism** – One or two persons of the Trinity are somehow less divine, or permanently ordered under the other persons.
- **Tritheism** – There are three separate Gods of Father, Son, and Holy Spirit.
- **Partialism** – Each person of the Trinity is only partially God.
- **Docetism** – Jesus is only divine and not human; he merely appeared to be human.
- **Macedonianism** – The Holy Spirit is created and not really God like the Father and Son.
- **Modalism** – God is one person only, with three distinct modes of being or expressions in history.

Every position on the rim holds some truth, but partial truth is imbalanced and misleading. Errors in understanding the Trinity often result from wanting to make sense of the Trinity by doing away with paradox. The positions on the rim are admittedly less paradoxical than the center. It is therefore difficult to hold the center, yet staying there or moving back, should you get caught on the rim, is the key to correctly understanding Jesus and the Trinity. Unless of course, you do not believe that the New Testament implies these paradoxes. Then this picture may not be worth a thousand words to you. Yet I would be hard pressed to see how such an interpretation is Jesus centered.

| LIVE LIKE IT MATTERS |

So what kind of heretic are you? Nobody holds a perfect balance all the time. Find yourself on the rim of misunderstanding. Which misunderstanding are you partial to? Cars need occasional alignment, and so does our thinking. Find your misalignment on the rim. Please do not beat yourself up over it or get defensive, but ask yourself with curiosity, "Why do I believe this?" Maybe you have good reasons for doing so, or maybe you don't. What does it look like to move back into balance and paradox? I believe that moving back to center will enlarge your perspective on God and move you to a place where the Trinity is a more powerful reality in your life..

11 EVERY CENTURY'S FAVORITE HERESY

Arianism and subordinationism are popular, but they miss the point of Christianity.

In Jesus, God chooses to identify with us in our humanity. The issue we face is whether we relate to God through Jesus because he is himself fully human and fully God, or if we relate to God through Jesus because he is something in between, *neither* human nor God, a middle man or conduit through whom we access the real deal. In a nutshell, this is the choice between orthodoxy and Arianism, between self-giving love and lording over each other in subordination, between faith in the Trinity and throwing Christianity out as offering nothing different from other religions. If the Son is a bridge being, then we have no revelation of God as a human in Jesus Christ. Yet if the Son is both God and human, then rather than being the bridge, he eliminates the chasm altogether.

Jesus is the way, the truth, and the life,[21] but the shocking claim of the Trinity is that in Jesus we come into relationship with the Father and Spirit because Jesus is united with them. The three are one. We do not come to the Father through Jesus because he is a go-between or a watered down version of God. If this was the case then the three could not be one. After claiming to be the way, the truth, and the life, Jesus in the very next verse explains, "If you know me, you will know my Father also. From now on you do know him and have seen him."[22]

If we lose this revelation of Godself in the human Jesus, we lose the Christ of Christianity. Historically, it was Arianism that worked so hard to lose the Christ of Christianity. Today, subordinationism, Arianism's little brother, has largely taken Arianism's place. Subordinationism is popular and appealing and we must now address it. Whenever one person of the Trinity is defined as more (or less) God than another, then you have subordinationism. It literally means to permanently order or rank one person below another—to

---

[21] John 14:6
[22] John 14:7

subordinate.

Even people who profess to believe in the equality of the Trinitarian persons may still subordinate Jesus to the Father. A contemporary evangelical argument stems from the desire to base on the Trinity the subordination of women to men. It claims that Jesus is to the Father *equal in being, but subordinate in role.* Kevin Giles sums up the problem with role subordination.

> Role subordination, we are told, does not imply inferiority. This is generally true, but once the note of permanency is introduced and competence is excluded, this is not true. If one party is forever excluded from certain responsibilities— no matter what their competency may be—simply on the basis of who they are, then this indicates they lack something that only their superior possesses. In other words, they are inferior in some essential way.[23]

If Jesus has less divine authority *eternally,* then the divine equality is false. This Arian current of thought within Christianity is widespread. Colin Gunton has referred to Arianism as "the 20th century's favorite heresy."[24] I think it is every century's favorite heresy, and honestly, I'm annoyed by it. It denies tri-unity for a unity in name only. It implies that Jesus and the Spirit are not really God. This sets up either levels of divinity that we need to work through (Gnosticism), or denies that we are indeed saved by God and indwelled by God. The result is that Christianity's claims of God's action in the world are false. The "real God," the Father alone, is too distant in eternity for relationship.

But why should we not accept that subordination exists in the Trinity?[25-26] Jesus himself said, "The Father is greater than I."[27] How

[23] Giles, *The Trinity and Subordinationism,* 17.

[24] Gunton, "And in One Lord Jesus Christ ... Begotten Not Made," *Pro Ecclesia* 10, no. 3 (2001), 261.

[25] For a defense of subordinationism, see Craig S. Keener, "Is Subordination Within the Trinity Really Heresy? A Study of John 5:18 in Context," *Trinity Journal* 20, no. 1 (1999).

[26] For another defense of subordinationism, see Stephen D. Kovach and Peter R. Schemm Jr., "A Defense of the Doctrine of the Eternal Subordination of the Son," *Journal of the Evangelical Theological Society* 42, no. 3 (1999).

can we argue with that? From his conception to resurrection, Jesus is completely dependent upon the power of the Holy Spirit. And if the three divine persons of the Trinity are all equally God, how then is each unique, and how do we reconcile their submission that we see witnessed to in Scripture? We will get to these questions shortly.

Not all subordinationists are Arians—believing that the Son is created—but practically they have the same effect. They share the same premise that the Son is not fully God, therefore the Trinity is not a Trinity. The functional result is that Christianity becomes no different from Judaism or Islam, Jehovah's Witnesses or Mormonism. They all think that Jesus and the Spirit are great, they just don't think they are God! A subordinated Jesus and Spirit have no divine power, purpose, or presence. Sure, the Father can empower anyone at anytime, can send any "divine" messenger at any time. That's exactly how Islam and Judaism work without the Trinity. Christianity is something else entirely, and it is something that subordinationists do not like.

Jesus is Emmanuel—God with us—because he is truly human *and* truly God. Remove either and there is no Emmanuel. As we saw in Philippians 2, Christianity is faith that Jesus is in very nature God and is equal to God. The Son shares perfect equality with the Father and the Holy Spirit. In order to become human, he gave up the functional power and privileges of divinity. Being human, he submitted to the Father in dependence upon the Holy Spirit. He "humbled himself by becoming obedient to death."

Jesus does not exist eternally in this lesser state; he assumed this state temporarily. Hebrews 2:9 says that the Son "was made a little lower than the angels," meaning he became human—which is why as a human he says that "the Father is greater than I." Hebrews 5:8 makes this more explicit, stating that Jesus "learned obedience through what he suffered." As a human Jesus had to *learn* obedience to the Father. Before Jesus became human he was functionally God alongside the Father—a position not requiring obedience, or learning obedience, but mutual submission in love. If non-mutual submission

---

[27] John 14:28

and obedience to the Father is part of the Son's eternal state, then he would not have had to "learn" obedience.[28]

The humbling of Jesus from his birth to his crucifixion does not make him any less God. These humiliations happened in time and are overcome in time through the resurrection and ascension. At the incarnation, Jesus never stopped being God. The being of God did not change from divine to human; rather in Jesus we see what God is like as a human. God is willing to accommodate us and take on our humanity out of love. What the incarnation accomplishes is the temporary lowering of the Son so that we can eternally be lifted up.

This is the Good News. In God's free choice to lavish us with grace, he takes on our sin, suffering, and death so that through faith we may share in his resurrection and eternal life. Our God of love does not hesitate to lower himself to serve and save others. That's just who God is. It doesn't make God any less God to do so. We therefore shouldn't think of the Son as subordinate to the Father. The Son's actions are just as godly as the Father's and indeed of the Spirit's. And in one, we always find the others.

| LIVE LIKE IT MATTERS |

Let's not forget the Holy Spirit! If we do not believe that the Spirit is fully God, then we are unlikely to believe that we can be transformed by the Sprit within us. The commands of Jesus are difficult to follow, and they require a belief that the Spirit can empower us to do what seems impossible. With a low view of the Spirit, we end up with a low view of ourselves and what God can do in us. What command of Jesus seems impossible for you now? Pray that the Holy Spirit would enable you to live into this command. How are you being challenged to love? You have everything you need to succeed—you have God within you! He wants to transform you by his power, and you can't do it through your own.

---

[28] Gilbert Bilezikian, "Hermeneutical Bungee Jumping: Subordination in the Godhead," *Journal of the Evangelical Theological Society* 40, no. 1 (1997).

12   THE HOLY SPIRIT WALKS INTO A COFFEE SHOP

Who is God, Spirit, and also a real person? The Holy Spirit.

When I was in seminary, I worked as a barista at a trendy, somewhat snobby coffee bar in Seattle. The advertised store policy was to ignore any customers who were rude or on a cell phone—a newly popular item at the time. If I wanted to, I could treat customers as if they didn't exist, and if they demanded attention I could point to the sign that explained my treatment of them, and ask the next person in line to order. This usually had one of two effects. Either the person came to a realization of his behavior and then perhaps apologized, or the person would get defensive and furious. When we got an angry reaction, we would simply act as if he or she wasn't there at all.

How I treated these customers is often exactly how we treat the Holy Spirit—we ignore him. He might tag along as an accessory to Jesus or the Father, but he isn't a person we notice. He may as well not really exist. Church theology usually doesn't help, often relegating the Spirit to some abstract notion, or else seeing the works of the Spirit as a rude interruption into our perfectly controlled settings. The truth is, like the customer at the coffee shop, most of us haven't treated the third person of the Trinity very well. Fortunately for us, he doesn't become defensive or furious!

It is difficult for us in the West to imagine the personhood of the Holy Spirit because we tend to characterize him by using our preconceived notions of "spirit" rather than by the personal and relational character of God. Yet in the Gospels Jesus refers to him with personal pronouns.[29] The Holy Spirit is not an impersonal force; he is an essential person of the divine communion. God does not exist apart from the Spirit, and we do not have relationship with God apart from the Spirit. A high view of the Trinity demands a high view of the Holy Spirit that sees him not as the byproduct of the Father and Son but as the real, present, and fully divine third person of the Trinity.

---

[29] John 14–16

Since St. Augustine expounded on the idea, it is popular in Western Christianity to say that the Holy Spirit is the bond of love between the Father and the Son. This is true, but only within the broader Trinitarian symmetry we often ignore. God is love, and this love involves the mutual submission of persons. The Holy Spirit is not divine mayonnaise holding the Father-and-Son sandwich together. Rather, it is the Father, Son, and Holy Spirit's interpersonal communion that constitutes the singular being of agape love that *is* the Trinity. The three persons of the Trinity are therefore equally and dynamically the bond of love that constitutes Godself. God is not a binity of Father and Son in which the Holy Spirit is merely the link, bond, byproduct, or some accessory between them. The Spirit is not a divine force. He is not simply a conduit through which we have a connection with the Father and the Son.

At the coffee shop, we liked to be in control of the atmosphere, which is why we treated some customers the way we did. And we tend to do the same to the Holy Spirit. So in our churches we create systems that acknowledge his presence under our own rules and in our own time. Since the ascension of Jesus, it is the Holy Spirit who is most immediate to us in time and space. He is not here in the flesh as a particular person, because his desire is to represent Jesus universally in all times and places at once. The simple fact is that we can't have relationship with God except through the Spirit. In fact, it is he whom we experience directly when we encounter God. And an encounter with the Spirit is an encounter with a person beyond our rules, beyond our assumptions, and beyond our control.

The shape this encounter takes cannot be boxed in any more than the personhood of God can be boxed in. Churches like to prescribe how the Spirit acts in the world and in your life. Sometimes these prescriptions are cessationist: They look in Scripture at a past action of the Holy Spirit and say, "Well, God doesn't do that anymore; that has ceased." Other times the prescriptions are more charismatic: They lay out a life you must be living and the rules you must follow in order to experience supernatural phenomena or "charisma."

The scriptural witness is not one in which prescribed rules are placed on the Spirit. We often mistake the Spirit for a divine force operating under certain cosmic laws, in the way that gravity operates under certain physical laws. The truth is that the person of the Holy Spirit can be known,[30] but he cannot be controlled.[31] Attempts at controlling the Holy Spirit usually involve a one-size-fits-all approach as to what relationship with the Spirit looks like. This is likely to entail rigid norms governing spiritual gifts, outward behavior, and inward feeling or emotion. What the Trinity reveals to us is that the only limit on the behavior of the Holy Spirit is the limit of God's unchanging character.

So how is the Spirit at work in the world? We know that the Father, through the Son, has sent the Holy Spirit to be with us,[32] and it is through the Holy Spirit that Jesus continues to be with us.[33] A direct *physical* relationship with Jesus is not currently possible, for he has ascended to heaven, and he has not yet returned in glory.[34] Yet we have not been left alone,[35] for the Spirit is among us presently and personally,[36] and through him we encounter the Father and the Son. Jesus did not give us a comforter who is not present, but someone who is more real than the person sitting across from you at the coffee shop!

Unlike Jesus, who took on a limiting human form, the Spirit is everywhere at once and not confined to a physical body. The Spirit has been placed in our hearts,[37] intercedes for us in prayer,[38] is present in worship,[39] empowers us with spiritual gifts,[40] grows the fruit of the Spirit within us,[41] and is with the Church even to the end

---

[30] John 14:17
[31] John 3:8
[32] John 20:22
[33] 2 Corinthians 3:17–18
[34] Acts 1:6–10
[35] John 16:7–8
[36] John 14:17, Romans 8:9, 1 Corinthians 3:16, 6:19, 2 Timothy 1:14
[37] 2 Corinthians 1:22, Galatians 4:6
[38] Romans 8:26
[39] Philippians 3:3
[40] 1 Corinthians 12:4, Hebrews 2:4
[41] Galatians 5:22–23

of the age.[42] As we worship in the Holy Spirit, we anticipate the same Spirit who will bring about the reconciliation of all things upon the eschaton. In worship we participate in this reconciliation with God by allowing the restorative work of the Spirit to transform our lives and to bring about a new creation in and around us.

People often wonder: If the Holy Spirit is a person, why do we not get a sense of his personality? This is because the Spirit points only to Jesus. And unless John 1:14, Colossians 1:15, and Hebrews 1:3 are wrong, it is Jesus who perfectly reveals God's character to us. While God is revealed as three persons, God does not have three separate personalities like popular culture might think. It is not as if the Father is mean, the Son is kind, and the Spirit is mysterious. Jesus perfectly represents God for us, and in doing so he reveals exactly what the Father and Spirit are like. Just as Jesus points us only to the Father, so too the Spirit points us only to Jesus. To come full circle, I like to think that in creation the Father only points us to the Spirit. It is the Spirit who initiated creation, will bring it to perfect restoration at the end, and currently groans within creation for its liberation in Jesus.

The Holy Spirit is presently doing the work that the Bible calls sanctification.[43] To sanctify means to make holy. You can think of it simply as restoration to what we were always created to be. It is the continuation of creation and redemption, part of the ongoing dance of the Trinity. It is God's saving action in the world that brings all things into their God-intended fullness. All of creation and all of time are concerned here, along with you and me.

Being a person who exists as an act of divine communion along with the Father and Son, the Spirit is deeply relational and concerned with your person and your relationships. This is why Scripture says that we can see his work in the world through the fruit of the Spirit in each other.[44] The role of the Holy Spirit in the world is no less than the sanctification of the universe, and we partner with him in that

---

[42] John 14:26, Matthew 28:20
[43] 2 Thessalonians 2:13, and 1 Peter 1:2
[44] Matthew 7:15–20, Galatians 5:22–23

work now by cultivating love, joy, peace, patience, kindness, goodness, faithfulness, gentleness and self-control *within* each of us, and *between* human persons in relationship. In the person of the Holy Spirit, God walks into the coffee bar every day. His constant presence is a comfort, but for us humans, who can prefer not to live in the light, he can be uncomfortably present.

| LIVE LIKE IT MATTERS |

It's commonly advised that you put your phone away when spending time with friends and family. Do this! It's also a good idea to schedule some Holy Spirit time without your screens. Spending time with the Spirit is nothing magical—he's always with you, and it is a great way to do what Jesus calls "abiding in me." Try one of the following: walking outside, doing yoga, reading Scripture, meditating, or just sitting down mindfully with a cup of coffee (or tea or whatever). Don't try too hard, just be present. And listen. As Paula D'Arcy is famous for saying, "God comes to you disguised as your life." And by life, I'm guessing she didn't just mean technology and social media.

13 LOVE, RIGHT THINKING, AND OTHER RELIGIONS

Can we get a little orthopraxy with our orthodoxy?

When I was teaching a class on the Trinity at my church in Pennsylvania, a former Mormon remarked on how difficult it was for her to leave the Mormon Church—not because of its unorthodox views on the Trinity, but because of how well they loved her and seemed to love those around them. Mormons are a prime example of people who tend to outperform the average Christian when it comes to loving our neighbors as ourselves. I believe it is largely because of this that they are one of the fastest-growing religions in North America, if not the world.

This is not surprising, for Jesus said that the world would know his disciples by our love for one another.[45] All this proves a very uncomfortable point for high Trinitarians such as myself: Since the Trinity is love, it is in the rightness of our actions—how well we love—not the rightness of our beliefs, that matters in evangelism. Right action (orthopraxy), is integral to right belief (orthodoxy). If you want your neighbors to be more orthodox like you, then start acting more orthoprax[46] like Jesus!

In general it seems clear to the world that Christians on the whole live no better, and love no better, than the non-Christians around them. Our fear-driven version of the Gospel is often a shadow of the whole Gospel, and like weak views of the Trinity, it can be fatally incomplete. "Beloved, let us love one another, because love is from God; everyone who loves is born of God and knows God. Whoever does not love does not know God, for God is love."[47] Yes, there are eternal, hellish consequences for rejecting God's love. This is all the more reason why our focus should be on reflecting and extending this love, showing ourselves to be true followers of God.

My wife and I have spent the last 10 years studying, teaching and developing discipleship ministries. One thing we've noticed is that

---

[45] John 13:35
[46] Orthoprax is not a real word. Use with caution.
[47] 1 John 4:7–8

fear-based conversions often attract people who are resistant to love and transformation. We can't easily grow into love when responding in fear. Behavior modification can work for a time, but it inevitably fails to transform us when we are grounded in fear instead of focusing on who God is as self-giving love. "There is no fear in love, but perfect love casts out fear; for fear has to do with punishment, and whoever fears has not reached perfection in love."[48] Of course, none of us has yet reached such perfection, but for the world to see Jesus and want to follow him, we all should be in the business of being transformed by God's love, and then showing it.

More than just the mind is involved when it comes to faith; it is the entirety of our being—heart, soul, mind, and strength. Agreeing with the right theology is not enough. When people hear that I have a degree in microbiology, the nearly universal response is to ask if I am a germophobe. Yet my degree in microbiology has not made me more germ-conscious, as one might think. Rather, it has had the effect of desensitizing me to the ubiquitous nature of pathogens. I am so desensitized that I am more likely to act as if they do not exist, despite my better-than-average knowledge about them.

Knowledge and even experience do not alone transform a person. In Romans 12 we are taught that being transformed by the renewing of our minds *comes after* offering our bodies as living sacrifices. This renewing is followed by becoming able to test God's good, pleasing, and perfect will. We wish the sequence were the other way around (know God's will, be transformed, then live with sacrificial love), but then it would not be faith. With all true faith, sacrificial love comes first, transformation second, and knowledge of God last. Thankfully, they come in quick succession. It is like getting married or having a child. *Without first giving yourself over to sacrificial love, transformation and insight from God are not very forthcoming. Why? Because you are not open to God, who is love.*

It then makes perfect sense that what we profess about the Trinity rings hollow when we fail to live into the life of love that the Trinity extends. I am preaching to myself here, for this book makes

---

[48] 1 John 4:18

clear that I place a very high value on right thinking. I have already mentioned how our weak understandings of the Trinity result in a godless Christianity that has no value or uniqueness compared to other religions. I am convinced of the importance of a particularly strong, integrated, and egalitarian view. It is my passion. And I encourage you to pursue your own similar intellectual passions.

Yet all of us must remember that even if we have a theology that can move mountains and bring crowds to tears of joy, if we do not have love, we have nothing. May we be inspired by the Spirit to move past theological disputes and love as Jesus demonstrated. May our faith in Jesus empower us to pour ourselves out in love. In turn the promise is that we will be filled with the eternal life of the Trinity. In other words, if you believe in the Trinity, then start acting like it by loving your neighbor, pouring yourself out for others, and receiving love in return!

| LIVE LIKE IT MATTERS |

It's time to get down to brass tacks and love someone we'd rather not. Only you know who that is. That neighbor you wish would move away? That coworker who makes your life miserable? The family member who is "literally" the worst? I'm not advising that you be a doormat or don't have good boundaries. I am saying that if you think hard enough, someone will come to mind. And if you think a little harder, what you should do to love that person will come to mind. It might make you feel good, or it might make you feel sick just thinking about it, but let's be followers of Jesus and love even the unlovable. He did it for us. I recommend you write down what you will do, for whom, and when. Write it down in this margin if you like. Don't miss an opportunity to grow into the knowledge of God!

PART II

WHEN AND WHERE MATTERS

14 BUTTER, JESUS, AND THE TRINITY

With apologies to vegans for this greasy analogy.

I hate trying to spread cold butter, especially on soft bread. Cold butter is a recipe for tearing, clumping, and general frustration. However, warm butter changes everything. I also dislike spreading cold butter with a spoon—yes, I have done this and even wilder things in my life, if you can believe it. The right tool, be it culinary or theological, changes everything.

A Jesus-centered way of looking at the Trinity changes everything. Imagine clarity on issues of the Trinity, the dual nature of Jesus, eternal life, and the Holy Spirit. And imagine that the practical arguments of our time were informed simply and effectively by this clarity. When it comes to political issues of church leadership and sex roles, or deeper issues such as the human soul, free will, and sin, it often feels as if we are trying to spread frozen butter with a spoon. The paradox of Jesus is the knife, and the paradox of the Trinity adds the heat that slices through the butter. But to get this warm butter, we will first need to deal with an artifact of subordinationism in our theology—the eternal and temporal "trinities."

When I'm talking about butter, I'm talking about theology, of course! It is an awkward metaphor, but I think that you'd agree that our Trinitarian theology is often cold and stale. When warmed, it can certainly make eating the bread of life more appealing. We'd rather have a real piece of buttered bread than read a book about the Trinity, and for good reason—because we've separated the two paradoxes of Jesus and the Trinity, making Trinity talk nonsensical and not relevant to faith in Jesus. We've removed the core revelation of Jesus as fully human and fully divine from the core revelation of Jesus expressing God's perfect triunity.

These paradoxes must be brought together, but they were separated for a reason, which is that together they imply a contradiction: Jesus' perfect humanity is eternally linked to God in Jesus, bringing humanity terribly close to God. This is a big theological problem; in fact it has been *the problem* of theology since

God was born incarnate in Jesus, for humanity and God simply are not to be equated! We need a God who transcends humanity, history, and time-space, or else we do not actually have God at all.

The problem also happens to be *the solution*, for the belief that humanity is eternally linked to God in Jesus is something that we Christians, using the language of Jesus himself, like to call *eternal life*. It is the life and love of the Trinity overflowing to us in time. Without the two paradoxes of Jesus and Trinity living together, we don't have eternal life. If Jesus isn't *fully God*, then God has never been revealed among us, died to save us, or risen victorious from the grave. Yet if Jesus isn't *fully human*, then God has never taken on our humanity, borne our sin and shame, and triumphed over our enslavement. We are stuck between a rock and a hard place, and some warm, greasy butter is just the thing we need.

We've tried eliminating the paradoxes, and we've tried to keep the paradoxes apart to protect God from contamination with humanity and the decaying effects of time. My proposal is that we cross-link the paradoxes. Jesus defines the Trinity, and the Trinity defines Jesus. After all, being one with the Father and the Holy Spirit was Jesus' own self-understanding. Jesus reveals the real Trinity—not some Greek notion of a God who is unrelated, but the actual Trinity who relates to us in time and who exists in eternal communion.

This Christ-centered perspective is an embrace of two paradoxes that the Church has always taught. Holding them together is the challenge. Yet when we do so, we will find that historically impossible issues such as God's timelessness vs. God's temporalness, free will vs. predestination, and egalitarianism vs. subordinationism are simple to resolve, and even practically relevant. Better yet, we find an ethic of Jesus that not only informs the answers to all of our social problems of identity and power, but could even prevent such problems in the first place. That is some butter worth spreading around.

| LIVE LIKE IT MATTERS |

Without the Trinity, Christianity loses what makes it different from other religions and worldviews. Yet much of Christianity today has only a superficial Trinitarian faith. Here is a tip for deepening your perspective: When you are reading Scripture, praying, or just thinking, make Jesus and Spirit synonyms for God. Simply replace the word with "God." We have been trained to do this automatically with the Father, but not so much with the Son and Spirit. As you do so, your idea of God will be shaped and broadened in a triune way. Who knows—it might even make you smarter.

15 PUTTING TIME AND SPACE IN THEIR PLACE

Time and eternity are distinct, by definition and by God's design. However, they come together as one in Jesus.

As a young boy, I would give heaven quite a bit of thought, but thinking about forever is taxing. I certainly couldn't feel or comprehend what *billions* of years would be like, let alone infinite years, and trying felt a little bit like hell. I now think that my failure was not my inability to imagine infinite quantity (time stretching into infinity), but my inability to grasp that the story of the Bible is a story in which time, as an integral part of finite creation, has a definitive beginning and end. *As hard as imagining forever and ever is, it is even more difficult to understand that at the end, time, as we know it, will cease to be.*

Time and space are created. They begin at the moment of creation.

> "In the beginning when God created the heavens and the earth, the earth was a formless void, and darkness covered the face of the deep, while the Spirit of God swept over the face of the waters. Then God said, 'Let there be light'; and there was light. And God saw that the light was good; and God separated the light from the darkness. God called the light Day, and the darkness he called Night. And there was evening and there was morning, the first day."[49]

Once light and darkness are separated, that is, once space itself is created, time begins as well: "And there was evening and there was morning, the first day."

Scientists tell the story differently with the big bang theory and general relativity. While science attempts to answer the "what" and "how" of time-space, the creation account in Genesis is more concerned with the "who" and "why."[50] The scientific story is one in which time and space comprise a single four-dimensional fabric

---

[49] Genesis 1:5
[50] John H. Walton, *The Lost World of Genesis One*, (Downers Grove, IL: InterVarsity Press, 2010).

called time-space. The biblical and scientific stories converge in that time and space are part of a whole that theologians call creation. A few smart Christians and scientists disagree that time exists integrally with space as one "fabric" of time-space—perhaps time existed before the big bang in some way—yet the majority of physicists tell us that time and space begin together at the initial moment of creation they call the big bang, and that it is completely meaningless to conceive of time before it, or beyond the time-space it initiated.

More important, Scripture implies that an eternal realm exists in God beyond creation. While classically this was thought to be a *time-less* eternity, science has further suggested with quantum mechanics and string theory that God's transcendence *may* rather, or also, include extra time-space dimensions unavailable to us—a *time-full* eternity.[51] Since the human Jesus is God, we can add that God in Christ is somehow "time-full" within our four conventional dimensions as well.

Yet even if we assume some form of God's time-fullness, the Bible speaks of things that "God destined for our glory *before time began*,"[52] and ascribe to God "glory, majesty, power, and authority, *before all time* and now and forever."[53] And explain how God's "grace was given to us in Christ Jesus *before the ages* (times eternal)."[54] And how we can live "in the hope of eternal life that God, who never lies, promised *before the ages (times eternal) began*."[55] So whether God's transcendence is time-full or time-less, Scripture demands that God is somehow beyond the time-space he created—beyond even possible extra dimensions or other universes that may transcend or precede our own. As the Bible teaches, the eternal life God has purposed for us in Christ was chosen before creation—or before time in its created and historical sense even existed.

So I suggest first that time, like space, is a part of creation.

---

[51] Hugh Ross, *Beyond the Cosmos*, (Colorado Springs, CO: NavPress, 1999), 73-79.

[52] 1 Corinthians 2:7, NIV (italics mine)

[53] Jude 1:25 (italics mine)

[54] 2 Timothy 1:9 (italics mine)

[55] Titus 1:2 (italics mine)

Second, I put forward that eternity is beyond time, and not merely infinite time. *By time I do not mean merely sequence or even the measurement of it, but time in its fullest sense, where it is the substrate for all human history and integral to created time-space.* It is only in this fullest sense that I believe that God transcends time, for it seems reasonable that God can experience sequence within the interpersonal communion that constitutes the one being of God. Of course God is also within time in some way—the incarnation of Jesus demands this—but to be Creator, God must also be beyond it. It's paradoxical.

As a child, I would also try to imagine the infinite time of God's existence before creation, but prior to creation there simply is no time at all that we know of or can meaningfully speak of. Space and time have a definitive beginning, before which there was no time-space, only God. Space and time also come to an end (as we know it) at the eschaton, the return of Christ and the moment when time reaches its ultimate fulfillment in what the apostle Peter describes in Acts as the "universal restoration."[56] Revelation 21 and 22 describe how after the final judgment the heavenly city will descend to earth and consummate created space. This is what is often referred to as "the end of time."

> Then I saw "a new heaven and a new earth," for the first heaven and the first earth had passed away, and there was no longer any sea. I saw the Holy City, the new Jerusalem, coming down out of heaven from God, prepared as a bride beautifully dressed for her husband. And I heard a loud voice from the throne saying, "Look! God's dwelling place is now among the people, and he will dwell with them. They will be his people, and God himself will be with them and be their God. 'He will wipe every tear from their eyes. There will be no more death, or mourning or crying or pain, for the old order of things has passed away.' He who was seated on the throne said, "I am making everything new!" Then he said, "Write this down, for these words are trustworthy and true." He said to me: "It is done. I am the Alpha and the Omega,

---

[56] Acts 3:21

the Beginning and the End."[57]

Here the end of time is not an annihilation of time-space but a consummation in which creation is irrevocably altered and perfected through incorporation with eternity. There will be no more night, for darkness will be banished.[58] The sun and moon will no longer need to shine.[59] While the imagery should perhaps be taken metaphorically rather than literally, it serves to illustrate all the more just how completely different creation will be. Amazingly, there will no longer be separation between God and creation, nor between heaven and earth.

In common English usage, "eternity" has two definitions. The first defines eternity as "time without beginning or end," or infinite time. Yet this is far too small a picture of eternity. While mathematically valuable, infinite time is not large enough to be a biblical view. The second definition of eternity is that which is beyond time—beyond even infinite time. In the Bible, eternity is not bound by time as we know it, just as it is not bound by space as we know it—it implies something beyond. It transcends it in some meaningful way, or else God and creation would not be distinct. Yet distinct they must be, for God *created* time in its fullest sense, and *is* eternal in an uncreated sense.

We will get to how Jesus confounds and overcomes this classical definition in later sections, for in him we have a human who lived fully in time and space and who is also the eternal God. So while we are starting with a classical view, in Jesus our view will have to evolve. The entire witness of God's revelation in the Bible is one in which God acts to extend relationship to us *within* creation. How, then, can the eternal God with an absolute "position" outside of time be the relational, self-sacrificing God within time that Scripture witnesses to and that Jesus embodies?

One option is open theism. In this view the future is not settled,

[57] Revelation 21:1–6a (New International Version)
[58] Revelation 22:5
[59] Revelation 21:23

at least in large part for individual purposes, in that it hasn't happened yet for us or for God. Here, God chooses to not completely predestine or foreknow the future. In this view, time is not created as integral with space; time is merely sequence and how we experience change. The view that time is only the experience of sequence means that God does not exist outside of time, for sequence existed for God before creation in the interpersonal communion of love that is the Trinity. Since God experienced sequence before creation, and since creation itself is a "change in sequence," then for an open theist eternity is simply infinite time. Open theism readily explains free will and the problem of evil, and it is gaining in popularity.[60]

While classical theism clearly has its failings, which we will cover later, I am not yet totally convinced by open theism and its implication that time *is not* integral to space and that eternity *is* integral to created time. God can exist both within and beyond time simultaneously. I believe that the revelation of God in Jesus does not demand that we choose one or the other. A view of open theism I like, its implication of time and eternity aside, is argued by Greg Boyd. He proposes that God has exhaustive foreknowledge of the future but also gives us genuine free will (self-determining freedom). This means that God has exhaustive foreknowledge of nearly infinite future possibilities and has a sovereign, predetermined plan for each free will choice we can make, including how each choice fits in to his larger predestined story in Christ Jesus.[61] Here perfect free will and perfect foreknowledge combine in a multidimensional way.

Despite my openness to open theism, I wonder if open theism renders the incarnation of Jesus less meaningful. For if God already fully existed within time without the incarnation, then how do the incarnation, crucifixion, resurrection, and ascension of Jesus

---

[60] For a thorough overview of Christian open theism, see Gregory A. Boyd, *Satan and the Problem of Evil: Constructing a Trinitarian Warfare Theodicy* (Downers Grove, IL: InterVarsity Press, 2001). For a basic overview, see Gregory A. Boyd, *God of the Possible: A Biblical Introduction to the Open View of God* (Grand Rapids, MI: Baker Books, 2000).

[61] Boyd, *Satan and the Problem of Evil*, 116–144.

ontologically change creation (throughout time) to bring it all under Christ? It would still be a powerful witness to God's love for us, but it implies that God already bore the burden of sin and death within time before the cross. Perhaps this is the case, but does this reduce the cross from a historical and ontological necessity to merely a revelation of God's character, in which Jesus is just a nice example? I admit to not understanding these issues completely. My proposed solution is simple and paradoxical, based on the paradoxes of the dual nature of Jesus and the Trinity, with which Christians must wrestle anyway.

On the other end of the spectrum from open theists, classical theists use the dualism of time-space and eternity to separate God from creation—protecting God from attributes such as suffering, change, limited knowledge and power, etc. Since God knows and sees all of time from beginning to end by virtue of being in an absolute position outside it, God remains sovereign and pure. The problem is that in Jesus—and one could argue in the Trinity—God breaks those rules and exists within time-space as a suffering human who willingly gives up power. Others reject the dualism of classical theism and contend that God exists wholly within time, protecting God from behaviors such as overriding free will, predestining evil, being distant or dispassionate, etc. The problem here is similar, in that in Jesus, God breaks those rules and exists outside of time as the all powerful, pre-incarnate Word as well as the post-ascension Lord.

The story of the Bible begins with time's creation and ends with time and eternity coming together. Just as earth will be consummated by being incorporated into heaven, so too will time be consummated by being incorporated into eternity. This is the reconciliation of all things that is the final resolution of Scripture. This brings us to eschatological theism,[62] according to which the being of God is split into eternal and temporal with the coming of Jesus. The Father remains eternal, the Son becomes temporal, and upon the

---

[62] As variously espoused by theologians such as Jürgen Moltmann, Robert Jenson, Ted Peters, and Wolfhart Pannenberg.

resurrection and the eschaton, the Holy Spirit brings the being of God back together and while doing so incorporates time with eternity. Unlike my view in which the Son is paradoxically both eternal and temporal, with eschatological theism it is the Spirit who is both.

This is not the same as open theism, for while the future is open, the eschaton *determines* the past ontologically and retroactively, making it a reverse form of classical determinism; I call it post-determinism. It is also very close to Tri-theism, three separate Gods, in which Jesus is other to the Father. In my opinion, the strengths of eschatological and open theism can be maintained without their drawbacks if we find the integration of eternal and temporal primarily in the person of Jesus, rather than in the eschaton or in time itself. This solution both critiques and borrows from our present options—classical theism, open theism, and eschatological theism—resulting in a "Christological theism," if I may be so bold.

While it may not be philosophically in vogue then or now, I think it biblically accurate to see that eternity and time are distinct upon the act of creation, that in Jesus they come together as one in him, and upon the eschaton they come together as one for all. So we have time and we have eternity, and we have Jesus. And since Jesus is the exact representation of God's being, I would like to use him as our starting and ending points. You might be asking what wonky things such as time and eternity have to do with the Trinity. You see, we have inherited a problem, the temporal and eternal trinities. But first, a lighter chapter.

| LIVE LIKE IT MATTERS |

We live in four dimensions of time-space, but there is a lot more going on that we cannot see (whether it's beyond time-space or happening in additional dimensions within it). These days it is not religious people but scientists who are preaching on the reality of extra dimensions. While physicists try to figure it all out, the resurrected Jesus holds the here and now, as well as the beyond, together in his dual nature.

Science is simply a method of analysis, and because of humanity it can be biased and wrong, yet at its best science is the study of God's Trinitarian creation. So let's embrace science and learn about God through it. Where in nature or science do you find the Trinity at work? What field of study interests you? Geography? Biochemistry? Physics? Botany? Take a class or read a book on it. And do so prayerfully and worshipfully. Abiding with God can take on almost any form.

16 I NEED TO RELATE

Jesus must be fully human to be fully relatable. Yet he must be fully God to bear the weight of eternity.

I found myself back in Honduras in the summer of 2001. I had been there before, for two weeks during the previous summer. It was through the University of New Hampshire's chapter of InterVarsity Christian Fellowship, where I served in a medical team partnering with local doctors. We would go into the slums of Tegucigalpa or the remote villages of the surrounding mountains and give whatever medical and nutritional aid we could. We learned to bring lots of food with us, though for reasons other than you might suppose. You see, we couldn't stop the people we were trying to serve from giving us all they had out of hospitality. Feeling bad about it and also not wanting to get sick from food that might have microbes that our fragile stomachs couldn't handle, we would bring them a meal instead. Those two weeks changed my life forever. So I decided to go back the next summer.

This next time was completely different. A few recent college graduates, including myself, had joined a dozen or so current students and were spending a month there. We lived with upper-class Honduran students, rented a van and drove around half the country, building a few houses, seeing the sights, and studying Scripture. Through a contact, we ended up in the middle of nowhere in the mountains south of La Ceiba, where a group of missionaries lived. They farmed on steep hillsides and experimented with crops and farming techniques that they hoped would translate to a better life for those around them. We joined them for three days.

On the second day, our group leader led us in a Bible study on the temptation of Jesus. While not the point he was trying to make, he mentioned that Jesus, being God, knew the temptations beforehand and therefore knew what he would say in response to Satan. For some reason I was agitated by the idea of Jesus' foreknowledge and said something to that effect. How could it have been a real temptation if he knew it all ahead of time? I argued that this idea undermines Jesus' full humanity. It seemed that half of the group agreed with me and half with our leader, who was more concerned with Jesus' full divinity and his greater point—that Jesus, as God, had everything under control. For them, Jesus must always be fully God for his life, death, and resurrection to bear the weight of eternity. Thanks to me, our devotional time went on this rabbit hole for a while.

Eventually we got back on track, and we had a great time of prayer and fellowship. When we finished, we walked outside to a beautiful dusk, and I sat there on the hilltop. And I saw fireflies (or lightning bugs depending on where you are from), thousands of them—far more than I had ever seen in one place and time. I just had to stop and admire the beauty of it all. For a moment, in the middle of rugged country, we had found front-row seats to the beauty of God's creation. The lights flickered all around, and I felt that God was speaking to me.

I now know that Jesus gave up his divine privileges while remaining fully God. That he was just as human as you and I—more so, in fact, for his humanity was not corrupted by sin. He was truly tempted, yet he did not succumb to it. Through complete obedience to the Father and complete reliance upon the Holy Spirit, he was able to work divine miracles. At that moment in the summer of 2001, however, I simply felt that I needed a Jesus that I could relate to. And I can relate to him because he knows us truly and deeply. He is both ordinary like us and gloriously divine at the same time. He is God, and he is human, showing us how to be human. He has come to us in the flesh, yet his eternal light shines in the darkness, calling us to stop and pay attention, as the fireflies often do.

| LIVE LIKE IT MATTERS |

Jesus was truly tempted as we are, and he overcame. We can too when we are similarly empowered by the Spirit. I don't mean to pry, but what temptation are you struggling with now? I won't even list examples because I think you know what they are. Trust me, God can relate to your temptation because Jesus suffered and overcame it. And God has not given up on you because you've failed to resist. God is never the source of our temptation,[63] but he will use it to build us up. Invite the Spirit to empower you to overcome. Resolve to resist today. And tomorrow, do the same. Have grace for yourself, because God certainly does.

---

[63] James 1:13

17 TEMPORAL AND ETERNAL 'TRINITIES'

The classical view is on its way out, yet it leaves us with dual "trinities" and no one path to integration. The double paradox of Jesus is the key.

The classical tradition represents a God who is a-temporal, immutable, and omnipotent in whom the future is completely predetermined. Keeping God in this absolute position beyond time keeps the God of Greek philosophy simple, pure, and untouched by fallen creation and the destructive forces of time. Yet for Christians it has required having an additional Trinity that is derived from the timeless God—the Trinity of Scripture revealed to us as Father, Son and Holy Spirit.

This certainly puts the cart before the horse, in that our knowledge of God consists only of that which is revealed to us in time-space. If classical theologians are correct in that the eternal God is totally removed from time and unknowable by finite minds, then we cannot claim to know anything about this God, including the fact that this God is timeless, immutable, etc. More importantly, Jesus disproved the notion that God is unchanging, immaterial, and purely timeless. He lived fully in time and suffered as we do—and his full divinity, while distinguishable, is not separable from his full humanity.

The classical notion of God's timelessness needs revising in light of the Gospel. Jesus, a fully divine member of the Trinity, lived, died, and rose again in time, revealing that out of love for us, God chooses not to be absolutely timeless. Yet, since God created time-space, then God must be eternal in the sense that he is beyond time-space as well. Classical thinking segregated God from time because in time we experience chaos, decay, and death. *The ancient Greeks saw time as the problem, for within it they saw what science now calls entropy—continuing decay and ultimate death.* As they were pre-Christian, their mistake was associating such destructive forces with time in its narrowest definition—of passage or sequence itself, as opposed to the fallenness of the cosmos caused by sin. It is not sequence or even created time-space that causes death and decay, but as the fall makes clear, death and decay are caused by sin.

This might imply that the second law of thermodynamics, in which entropy increases over time, might itself be a result of cosmic sin. I'm not sure about this, but why not? After all, without God intervening, the fate of the universe is a cosmic heat death in which things spread themselves out into a static, maximally disorganized oblivion. The Bible tells a different story as to the ultimate fate of the universe. Whatever else the end of time entails, the eschaton will somehow be a moment when God once again breaks into time-space and reverses such entropy.

The scholarly consensus, starting in the mid 20th century, has slowly shifted away from the classical view in which God's timelessness is protected. Thomas Torrance sums up why:

> If the [temporal] Trinity and the [eternal] Trinity were disparate, this would bring into question whether *God himself* was the actual content of his revelation, and whether *God himself* was really in Jesus Christ reconciling the world to himself … If there is no real bond *in God* between the [temporal] Trinity and the [eternal] Trinity, the saving events proclaimed in the economy of the Gospel are without any divine validity, and the doctrine of the Trinity is lacking in any ultimate divine truth.[64]

In other words, *if the temporal Trinity we experience in our salvation as Father, Son, and Holy Spirit is not the same eternal Trinity, then there is no reason to assume that the Christian witness reflects God, that our Scripture is from God, and that our salvation is grounded in God.*

Classical thinking posits that while there is only one Trinity, we must think of God in two separate ways, or as two trinities: one in eternity and one in time. In theology these trinities each go by many different names.

The eternal Trinity, also called the ontological, theological, or immanent Trinity, or the Trinity *ad-intra*, is the triune God who exists in and for Godself from

---

[64] Thomas F. Torrance, *The Christian Doctrine of God: One Being Three Persons* (New York, NY: T&T Clark, 1996), 7–8.

all eternity, apart from the created world.

The temporal Trinity, also called the economic, evangelical, or functional Trinity, or the Trinity *ad-extra*, is God who is revealed to us in time-space as the Father, Son, and Holy Spirit. It is God for us in the economy of human salvation.

While not the common usage in theological texts, for the remainder of this text I will primarily use the terms "eternal" and "temporal" trinities. I prefer them, in that the terms are easier to understand, and we need all the help we can get.

The "eternal Trinity" is thought of as the transcendent God beyond time-space—the exclusive inner life of God. The "temporal Trinity" is our experience of God within time-space as revealed in the Scriptures as Father, Son, and Holy Spirit. It represents the outer life of God extended to us in the world. It is agreed that there is only one actual Trinity, but it is not agreed exactly what that entails. Is God paradoxically both fully within and beyond creation? Are eternity and time distinct, and if so, how? Should the submission of the Son to the Father in time be viewed as an eternal state of subordination? How can the two trinities be the same without collapsing God into the world in a type of pantheism that takes away God's freedom?

Compounding the issue, the Eastern and Western Churches each have a different take on the temporal and eternal trinities. And both East and West are conflicted regarding whether the Trinity is egalitarian (all equally God) or subordinationist (all not equally God). I've sketched on the following page how both the Eastern and Western Churches tend to understand the Trinity in relation to Godself and to the world. Recently, Christians in the West have been adopting the Eastern models as well. I will explain what some of the interesting differences are in later chapters. And I will offer a unified model that eliminates the problems and that incorporates the truth found in each of the models.

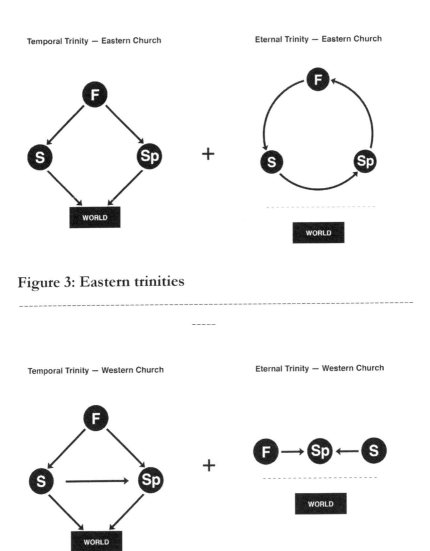

Figure 3: Eastern trinities

Figure 4: Western trinities

By embracing the double paradox of Jesus we can place the Trinity in the center of our faith with a unified perspective. It is easier, but not better, to keep the paradoxes separate, for bringing the two together implies that the human Jesus is simultaneously one being with the Father and Spirit. This might indicate that his humanity is in some way a part of the eternal being of God. If this idea makes you uncomfortable, then you can now relate to wanting two trinities!

The Gospel bears witness to what seems impossible—Jesus is one with the Father and the Spirit, and simultaneously fully God and fully human. Integrating the temporal and eternal trinities is a task full of pitfalls. I believe that it is best achieved in and through the dual nature of the Son. And this in turn will allow the Trinity to practically apply to how we should live. Integration of the trinities is elusive because the duality allows us to avoid several issues that any unified understanding needs to confront. I'm aware of four theological hazards as we attempt to bring all things together in Christ Jesus. For those of you who are tracking with me theologically and want to dive deeper, I recommend that you now skip to Appendix 1 (Four Hazards of Integration) and read that chapter before doubling back to here. For everyone else, next is a quick break with something more practical.

| LIVE LIKE IT MATTERS |

So how comfortable are you with the idea that Godself includes humanity? It gives some people hives and others warm fuzzies, but Jesus pushes back against both extremes. In him we cannot deny the link, yet we cannot say that one is the other, for Jesus has two natures (inseparable yet distinguishable), not one mixed up nature. You are not God, yet through Jesus, the Spirit of God is in you. You and God are not as separate as we are sometimes told.

If we take Jesus at his word, then we are capable of doing greater things than he did.[65] What might God be calling you to do that seems out of reach? Write a book? Call your estranged family member? Give ten percent of your income away? If the calling is from God, then you have everything you need to succeed. You have God!

---

[65] John 14:12

18   GOD, GENDER, AND COMMON HUMANITY

The Trinity breaks through all barriers of division. We should too.

Then God said, "Let us make humankind in our image, according to our likeness.". . . So God created humankind in his image, in the image of God he created them; male and female he created them.[66]

Just as each person of the Trinity is fully God, male and female are each fully human. A divine person has the divine being in full, just as a human person has the "human being" in full. That is the idea anyway—humans are not quite fully human in as much as we are denatured by sin—but the Good News is that Jesus has come to remedy our inhuman situation. Just as the being of the Trinity is the communion of the three persons, the being of humanity is, ideally, the communion of human persons, male and female. In fact, I believe that it takes all of humanity in loving community to adequately bear God's image, for we are created in the image of a communal God.

Both male and female reflect God, even as God is not limited by maleness and femaleness. There is a great diversity of opinion across generations and cultures as to what maleness and femaleness entail beyond the obvious biological distinctions. These diverse positions disagree on the details, yet they all see humanity as sexed, gendered, and enculturated, for that is what human persons are. It therefore comes naturally to us humans to view divine persons in the same way. This is a mistake, even idolatry, for we remake God in our own image. Multiple problems come when we project our own image of a sexed, gendered, and enculturated personhood back onto God. As Karl Barth's axiom has taught us: we can let the personhood of God define human personhood, but we cannot let our human personhood define God's.

Speaking of God's personhood, what about Jesus? He was

---

[66] Genesis 1:26–27

definitely male, so does this fact exclude female persons in some way? The answer is no. *While Jesus is a man, every biblical reference to the incarnation of Jesus speaks explicitly of God becoming human as opposed to becoming a man.*[67] It is compelling that the texts concerning Jesus' assumption of human form take great pains to name him as human, and not as man or male, when so much of the Bible is not concerned with gender inclusiveness—at all. The New Testament writers took what was at the time extraordinary measures in communicating that Jesus is a particular *human* representative of all people, rather than someone exclusively representing any one particular people group, be it then or now, Jew or Gentile, slave or free, male or female.

Contrary to the teaching of the Bible, chauvinists have used the masculine language found within it to inflict harm by stating that God is male or primarily reflects maleness. On the other side are feminists who advocate for a reframing in which we refer to God as "she." Does thinking of God as a woman do further harm or merely balance the scales? Compounding the issue is the move by some to substitute impersonal job descriptions such as Creator, Redeemer, and Sustainer for the personal titles of Father, Son, and Holy Spirit. Since English lacks gender-neutral personal pronouns, gender-neutral titles are used as a compromise.

Because the Trinity reveals that God is absolutely relational and profoundly personal, we lose essential personhood when we use impersonal titles over personal ones, whether or not they are gender-neutral. I think it better to see how the traditionally masculine titles can be inclusive of the female sex. The traditional titles should not be abandoned. Rather we should use alongside them the scriptural metaphors that emphasize the feminine qualities of God. A multiplicity of names, analogies, titles, and metaphors are used for God. We need them all, for no single human concept or word can grasp the essence of God. God goes even beyond all of them together.

Debating the maleness or femaleness of God is always a trap in that it forces

---

[67] Stanley J. Grenz and Denise Muir Kjesbo, *Women in the Church: A Biblical Theology of Women in Ministry* (Downers Grove, IL: InterVarsity Press, 1995), 205–06.

you to sex and gender God in your own image. Or it forces you to properly name God, who is by definition beyond properly naming. In the book of Exodus, Moses gets an interesting answer from God when he asks after the proper name of God.

> Moses said to God, "Suppose I go to the Israelites and say to them, 'The God of your fathers has sent me to you,' and they ask me, 'What is his name?' Then what shall I tell them?"

> God said to Moses, "I AM WHO I AM.[68] This is what you are to say to the Israelites: 'I AM has sent me to you.'"

> God also said to Moses, "Say to the Israelites, 'The LORD, the God of your fathers—the God of Abraham, the God of Isaac and the God of Jacob—has sent me to you.'

> "This is my name forever, the name you shall call me from generation to generation."[69]

Moses gets two answers to his question about God's name. The first—I AM WHO I AM—implies that God is far beyond the concept of what we call a proper name. The second—The Lord, the God of your fathers, God of Abraham, the God of Isaac and the God of Jacob—implies that God is understood and known not through a proper name, but through a relationship. *And this is God's name forever, the name we shall call him from generation to generation—a name beyond naming except in personal relationship.*

God has male and female qualities in that God is relational love that male and female both reflect. The Father is therefore neither male nor female, and neither is the Holy Spirit—they transcend and include both. The same must be said even for the Son. Jesus came incarnate as a man, yet to claim that his incarnation was not inclusive of female humanity is to eliminate the possibility of salvation for women. As the Cappadocian maxim states, "What Jesus did not assume in his humanity he did not redeem." Any sins he did not assume on the cross cannot be atoned for. Any aspect of humanity he did not assume cannot be resurrected with him. This is the

---

[68] Or "I WILL BE WHO I WILL BE."
[69] Exodus 3:13–15 (NIV)

teaching of Hebrews 2:14–18. If femaleness is not included in the person of Jesus, then nothing female will share in Christ's resurrection. I am not proposing that Jesus was in any way *biologically* female, but stating the following rule: *If Jesus did not assume a universal humanity, then God's saving action in Jesus is not universal in scope.*

If the particularity of Christ as male is held in priority over Christ as human (by either extreme feminists or extreme chauvinists), then what can be said of people of races, cultures, times, places, ages, and classes who are other than that of Jesus? Jesus was a Palestinian Jew of a certain socio-economic status in the first century. Does his humanness extend beyond those particularities, and can those who find themselves outside of such characteristics (everyone alive today) be saved? The answer of the Church is a resounding "yes!"

Jesus came to reconcile us to God and to each other, not to institutionalize our separation. In fact, the isolation we experience within and between the sexes is merely symptomatic of our isolation from God caused by sin. Biological sex is a very real boundary within humanity. So what of other boundaries such as race, status, culture, and time? Is not the boundary of the individual, which divides absolutely everyone from everyone else, even greater than the boundaries of sex and race? Since Jesus is an individual distinct from all other human persons, is there salvation for anyone?

Rather than viewing Jesus as the primary obstacle to salvation, the good news Christians believe is Christ overcomes our alienated condition. If the Son can bring together time-space and eternity, why then would sex or gender leave us in isolation? For in Christ there is neither Jew nor Greek, slave nor free, male and female.[70] The Holy Spirit bridges the separation between Jesus and every isolated human individual.[71] As Galatians continues, "God has sent the Spirit of his Son into our hearts."[72] We are one in Christ Jesus through the Holy Spirit.[73] The Gospel powerfully proclaims that our common

---

[70] Galatians 3:28

[71] *The Holy Spirit: Classic and Contemporary Readings*, ed. Eugene F. Rogers Jr. (West Sussex, UK: Wiley-Blackwell, 2009), 1.

[72] Galatians 4:6

[73] 1 Corinthians 12:12-13

humanity *in Christ* overcomes our separation.

So back to the question of whether we can refer to God as she. Yes we can. God transcends and reflects the feminine as well as the masculine. It certainly can be edifying for us to commune with God and reflect on her feminine character. But just because you can do something doesn't mean you should. Context is key. Love is paramount.

We must not un-tether ourselves from God revealed as Father, Son, and Holy Spirit. It is like a helium filled birthday balloon. It doesn't send the celebratory message if you stuff it in a box. Yet if you untie it from its anchor, it will simply float away. We should remain ever tied in, never tied down to tradition. So let's recognize how we all reflect the image of God, but let's not forget how our God breaks through all barriers of division, and if the Church is in Christ, it will do likewise.

| LIVE LIKE IT MATTERS |

God is the great I AM, but for Moses, God is also the God of Abraham, Isaac, and Jacob. We know God through our human relationships. For me, God is the God of my parents, my pastors, and my friends. He is the God of Julie, Tom, and Andy. Perhaps you are someone through whom God is known. I try to be an instrument of knowing God for my church, my family, and my daughter. It requires God in me, and me in God. Through whom do you know God? What relationships have helped you come to know God? And who are you helping come know God? It matters for eternity.

19 ONE WILL OR THREE WILLS?

The Garden of Gethsemane Question.

Perhaps you are wondering if the Trinity has one will, three wills, or a perhaps a mix of both? I mean, for a person to be a person, they need an independent will, correct? Actually, when it comes to God, no they do not. I would say the same applies for perfect humanity. An interdependent will is the godly ideal. Jesus demonstrated that perfect humanity involves a will submitted to God. Yet the passage where Jesus prays to the Father in the Garden of Gethsemane is often raised as the clearest scriptural support for separate wills. After all, Jesus seems to not desire what the Father wills when he prays "not what I will, but what you will." Does his prayer indicate either a division of Jesus' will from the Father's or a division of Jesus' own will?

In regard to Jesus having two separate wills, a human and a divine which might be in conflict, I would simply respond that this one passage is hardly convincing evidence compared to the whole of Scripture. Jesus is not two persons, but one person who is paradoxically human and divine. Hate paradox? Well, I don't see how Jesus being two persons really helps you out. The question of Jesus' will being separate from the Father's has more merit I think. Let's look at the passages.

Matthew and Mark word it slightly differently, but the essence is the same.

> Going a little farther, he fell to the ground and prayed that if possible the hour might pass from him. "*Abba*, Father," he said, "everything is possible for you. Take this cup from me. Yet not what I will, but what you will."[74]

> Going a little farther, he fell with his face to the ground and prayed, "My Father, if it is possible, may this cup be taken from me. Yet not as I will, but as you will."[75]

---

[74] Mark 14:35–36 (NIV)
[75] Matthew 26:39 (NIV)

In both cases, Jesus is stating that his desire (or will) is that if possible, he not go through the immense suffering of the cross. Yet he is very clear that his ultimate desire (or will) is that the Father's will be done. He is honest about how he feels, yet he trusts the Father. In that Jesus' will here is ultimately "not what I will, but what you will," Jesus' will is not separate from or opposed to the Father's, but it does seem to be submitted to, and perhaps somewhat disconnected from the Father's. It appears that Jesus as a human might not be all knowing regarding the Father's will. How can this be if the Trinity is one being?

Some people see the temporary lowering of Jesus here on earth and wrongly assume that Jesus is that way in eternity as well, leading them to believe that Jesus is not as divine as the Father. The Bible tells us otherwise. As Philippians describes it, when Jesus became human, he voluntarily lowered himself and gave up divine privileges, though he never stopped being fully God. So during his earthly ministry, Jesus was not all-powerful, and he was not all-knowing. He temporarily gave these divine privileges up in order to authentically be fully human, like us. This is why as a human Jesus was fully obedient to the Father and fully dependent upon the Holy Spirit.

Jesus said that we can do even greater things than he did if we too follow his example of obedience to the Father and dependence upon the Holy Spirit. The miracles, special knowledge, and power that he displayed came from the Holy Spirit working within his human limitations. Jesus is literally the way to God and to becoming our fully human selves. He shows us the way by becoming human. We can have communion with God in that Jesus has made it possible. Our will is not God's will, but if we follow Jesus as Lord, Teacher, and Savior, being obedient to the Father and dependent upon the Spirit, then our will becomes more and more aligned with God's own.

The invitation is to eternal life in God—eternal meaning not merely forever in quantity, but of the highest possible level in quality. At his birth, Jesus experienced a separation from the Father and the Spirit. At the cross, starting at Gethsemane, Jesus experienced a further separation as he prepared to take on all sin, suffering, death, and the demonic, and defeat them. This separation culminated at Christ's death, just after he proclaimed "My God, my God, why have you forsaken me!" Jesus clearly is experiencing separation, yet he is quoting Psalm 22, and he would have had it's hopeful, victorious ending in mind even as he uttered his last.

There is an eternal aspect of the cross. Yet the eternal quality is not that Jesus lowered himself, or that he died, or that he took on our sin, for these were all reversed within time itself with Jesus' resurrection and ascension. The eternal quality is God's victory over sin and death, making right relationship with God and eternal life possible for us!

The temporary *experiential* separation of the Son from the Father and Spirit is a real logical problem, though. How is it that the divine *being* itself remained whole, yet the Trinity experienced separation? It goes to the heart of the paradoxes that we need to accept as our starting point: God is one, and yet God is three. Jesus is fully God (and therefore of one will and being in the Trinity), and yet Jesus is also fully human (and experienced separation from God for our redemption). How is a mystery, but the doctrine is not. The double paradox of Jesus is the cornerstone of our faith, and it supplies abundant answers without revealing God's mysteries.

| LIVE LIKE IT MATTERS |

Feeling distant from God? So did Jesus, who paradoxically is God. What he models for us at Gethsemane is that it is good to be honest with God and others about how you feel. We see as much in the Psalms and other passages of Scripture, but in Jesus we find the ultimate model. Jesus expresses his emotions and desires, voicing them all night long! In doing so he submits them to the will of God. I know, the will of God is also his own will, and our wills are certainly not God's. Yet an amazing thing about faith in Jesus is that over time, our will can more and more become God's will. Try praying the Lord's Prayer with this in mind every day for a week.

20 JESUS: THE PROBLEM AND THE ANSWER

Jesus has always been a dilemma, as well as the solution to a God of relationship.

The full divinity of Jesus and the Holy Spirit have been hard to accept ever since Jesus announced the Kingdom of God. It was the belief in Jesus as God that forced the split between Judaism and Christianity. We like to call the apostle Thomas *doubting Thomas*, but that doesn't give him the credit he deserves, as none of the disciples believed in the resurrection until seeing the risen Jesus. When Thomas finally did see Jesus, it was he who gave the strongest proclamation of who Jesus is, exclaiming, "My Lord and my God!"[76] Thomas was among the first to believe what Jesus had been teaching; that he is Lord and God. This is blasphemy and nonsense from a Jewish perspective.

Jesus is not merely sent from God, but is God. "In the beginning was the Word, and the Word was with God, and the Word was God."[77] This vague notion avoids major controversy until we read on. "And the Word became flesh and dwelt among us."[78] God had entered human history in a profound way that was not anticipated. That this messiah was crucified without bringing political liberation was a stumbling block for many. Judaism could absorb Jesus as prophet, as have Islam and other faiths, but accepting Jesus as God was a leap that many Jews were not willing to make. *It was the claim that Jesus was not only human but also divine, a claim that led to belief in the Trinity, that caused Christianity to become a religious movement in its own right.*

Yet what was a stumbling block for the Jews was regarded as foolishness to the Greeks.[79] The incarnation of God in Jesus Christ was problematic because the God of the Greeks was static and unchanging, timeless, and unfeeling.[80] The pantheon of gods was

---

[76] John 20:28

[77] John 1:1

[78] John 1:14

[79] A paraphrase of 1 Corinthians 1:23

[80] Robert W. Jenson, *The Triune Identity: God According to the Gospel* (Eugene, OR: Wipf and Stock, 2002), 57–77. Elizabeth A. Johnson, *She Who Is: The Mystery of God*

seen as the necessary mediator between the two realms of God and humanity. That this "transcendence-only" God became flesh was offensive and impossible. By Jesus' time, the Hebrew people had lived for centuries under Greek and Roman rule, and their religion and philosophy was not sealed away from the influences of Hellenism—Greek philosophy and religion.[81] The claim that God had become a part of creation by becoming human posed a massive challenge for the Greek worldview. It was a challenge that the early Christian apologists were ready to meet.

Because Christians did not worship the pagan gods, they were charged with atheism. The Christian apologists responded that they worshipped the same God of the Greek philosophers. In essence, they claimed that the Father was the Monist God of the intellectual elites.[82] This apologetic proved successful over time,[83] but planted seeds that led to Arianism, the belief that the Son is created, as well as many of the other mistaken views on the outer rim (see Figure 2). The problem was that the Christian God and the Greek God was not really the same God in many important respects.

This eventually brought the Church to an impasse, resulting in the great Christological controversies of the fourth and fifth centuries. From these controversies came the creeds and the formal doctrine of the Trinity, in which the persons of the Son and the Holy Spirit were upheld as fully God along with the Father.[84] Yet the issue has not gone away.

The issue then and now is the absolute divinity of the Trinity versus the absolute divinity of the Father over and above the Trinity.

---

in Feminist Theological Discourse (New York, NY: Crossroad Publishing Company, 1992), 17–41.

[81] John Zizioulas, *Being as Communion: Studies in Personhood and the Church*, Contemporary Greek Theologians (Crestwood, N.Y.: St. Vladimir's Seminary Press, 1985), 17.

[82] Justin, (Apology c.150), I. xlvi, II. xiii. Clement of Alexandria (Stromateis c.200) I. v. 28 *Documents of the Christian Church*, ed. Henry Bettenson and Chris Maunder, Third ed. (Oxford: Oxford University Press, 1999), 5–7.

[83] Justo L. González, *The Story of Christianity: Volume I* (San Francisco, CA: Harper Collins, 1984), 56–57.

[84] For a brief overview on this see Ibid., 16–17, 52–57.

As disciples of Jesus we face a choice. Is God a perfect relationship of love both within and beyond time, revealed as the Trinity, implying that relational love is essential to who God is? Or is God eternally separate from us and the world, where Jesus and the Spirit are merely go-betweens?

Great thinkers on the left often reduce Jesus to an example or principle of what a godly life can look like. The *actual person* of Jesus becomes superfluous, for he merely exemplifies the ideal "Christ" potential that we all can tap into. Meanwhile, great thinkers on the right often reduce Jesus to *merely* God's Son, subordinating him to the Father while neglecting that the Son is himself fully God. In this view the person of Jesus remains important for our salvation, but distorted. Instead of the paradox of fully God and fully human, he becomes a bridge being in between God and humanity. This makes Jesus unable to relate to us human to human, and removes him from equality with God as God.

Jesus is indeed our example and our mediator. Yet Jesus is more than our example and more than our mediator. *He is our fellow human and our eternal God.* Truly transcending us as our God, yet truly identifying with us as a human, he is our Lord, Teacher, and Savior. In him is eternal life, the source of all relationship. Jesus is always the answer because Jesus is *the* answer. Jesus is God revealed, or as Hebrews chapter 1 states, Jesus is the exact representation of God's being who sustains all things.

Jesus is also the answer when it comes to an integrated model of the Trinity. He is the revelatory source of our knowledge of the Trinity, and he is God made flesh, the bond between time and eternity. He is therefore the key to integrating the temporal and eternal trinities. "For in him the fullness of God was pleased to dwell, and through him God was pleased to reconcile to himself all things, whether on earth or in heaven, by making peace through the blood of his cross."[85]

Rather than making Jesus fit into preconceived notions of God, we must define God through the teaching, life, and person of Jesus. Paradoxically, Jesus

---

[85] Colossians 1:19-20

points to God within himself, as well as beyond himself, yet always in unity with the Father and Spirit. It is the Father himself who addresses the Son directly in the Scriptures as "God" and "Lord."[86] It is in the birth of Jesus that for the first time since the Garden we truly had Emmanuel—God with us. It was at his baptism that the heavens were literally "torn open" so that the Spirit could descend and the Father speak his affirmation.[87] It was on the cross that God bore our sin and its consequences, and it was in the resurrection that the enemies of God and the forces of disintegration were dealt a decisive blow.

Jesus reveals a God who gets his hands dirty with creation. Lowering oneself in this way is in part what it means to be God. The Bible tells us that Jesus reveals God exactly (Hebrews 1:3), and that if we have seen Jesus, then we have seen the Father (John 14:9). The Hebrew understanding of God in the Old Testament is a God who acts personally in human history. In Jesus we have a God who not only acts in human history, but a God who physically becomes a human being. Through Jesus the separation between God and us is eliminated.

To say that this was counter-intuitive for the ancient Greek mind would be a gross understatement. Since Jesus and the Holy Spirit seemed to be more intimately related to creation, it was more natural for them to equate the Father with the God of Greek philosophy. This melding incorporated the best of Greek philosophy into the Christian faith, but understanding the Trinity within Hellenism was not stable.[88] It worked only as long as people were willing to ignore the inconsistencies between the Father as ultimately God, and Jesus and the Holy Spirit as God with the Father. The Arians were not so willing, and they desired to take the Hellenist gospel to its logical end. At the start of the fourth century the Church's first great controversy was exploding.

---

[86] Hebrews 1:5–13
[87] Mark 1:9-11
[88] Jenson, *The Triune Identity*, 125–26.

| LIVE LIKE IT MATTERS |

Are you more on the left, prone to view Jesus as just an example of the Christ potential in each of us, or are you more on the right, prone to view Jesus as merely a mediator of salvation between yourself and God? Both are true, yet alone they both reduce Jesus to something far less than he is—fully human and fully God. Jesus is more than Teacher, and more even than Savior. He is also Lord, meaning he has the authority to tell us how we should live. Is Jesus your highest authority? There is one way to tell: Are you acting more and more like him over time?

21 THE ARIAN REACTION

Arianism—a logical response to the Jesus problem.

To understand the Arian controversy of the fourth century and its effects for us today, we need to take a quick look back. The Arians used biblical texts to support their view that Jesus was not God, but was a creation of the Father. In Arianism, the Son is created prior to the world, and he then takes part in creating the cosmos under the direction of the Father. The Son is so superior to us that we can rightly call him "God," for he is a type of god, but in Arianism, Jesus is not actually God as the Father is. Educated people of the time were steeped in Greek philosophy, and they believed, among other problematic things, that God could not suffer in any respect, despite scriptural passages to the contrary. Arians believed that since Jesus suffered, he must be of a different being (or substance) from the Father.

In boldly proclaiming what was implied within the Christian-Hellenic compromise, Arianism argues that there are not three divine persons who are fully and equally one God. There is no real Trinity. With Arianism, God the Father is the God of the philosophical ideal—static, unrelated, and absolute. Arianism nicely unites monism with polytheism in that the Son and Holy Spirit are divine middlemen who are demoted to lesser gods that inhabit a realm between time and eternity. They are not God and yet not quite creatures like us— forming the link needed to bridge the divide between God and the world. *The practical difference is that with the actual Trinity, Jesus is the paradoxical link, in that he is fully God and fully human, while with Arianism Jesus is the logical link (from a Greek perspective) in that he is neither God nor human, filling the space between.*

Facing Arianism, the Christian leaders at Nicaea saw that Arianism was not the faith that had been handed down to them, nor the faith of the Scriptures. In their view the faith taught that the Son is God. He is not just a god relative to them, but God. Period. The ecumenical councils condemned Arianism, but it never really went away. A form of ontological subordination, Arianism states that the being of Jesus is less than the Father's. Subordinationism is Arianism's little brother because while it may claim that all three persons of the Trinity are equally God in their being, it denies such equality in their action. It is a philosophical distinction, but often one without a practical difference, for with both, Jesus and the Spirit are not functionally equivalent to God, and the actions of God in the world are not united, resulting in the being of God being divorced from the work of God in the world.

In fact, you might be an Arian and not even know it. It can happen to the best of us. I've been a part of churches of various denominations all across the United States. In each context, I've noticed something they have in common: Most people don't know what to think about the Trinity, despite professing belief in it. When people's guard is down, I hear comments such as, "I know that Jesus loves me, but it is hard to imagine that God does," or "Sometimes I pray to God, but other times I pray to the Holy Spirit." In their minds, God is synonymous not with the Trinity, but with the Father alone, even if they know that "Jesus and the Spirit are God, too." But such comments reveal that, in fact, they do not know what the Trinity is!

While Arianism is widely recognized as heresy (which before it came to mean something sinister, heresy simply meant *a divergent choice*), its lighter version, subordinationism, persists in the Christian mainstream, resulting in the confusion of the eternal and temporal trinities that has percolated down through every level. Christians are ambivalent and confused, and not wanting to get it wrong, they live precariously on the tightrope between Arianism and orthodoxy. The problem is that most of us aren't very good tightrope walkers. The first gust of wind sends us careening, and there is no telling on which side we'll land. Eternal or temporal? Egalitarian or subordinationist? I propose that we get off this tightrope altogether. Jesus walked it for us so that we don't have to.

| LIVE LIKE IT MATTERS |

It's time for us to think of Jesus and the Holy Spirit as synonymous with God. I've already suggested you try substituting "God" for Jesus or Spirit in certain passages of Scripture. You can even do it the other way around. It's true that often a particular verse has a certain member of the Trinity in mind when it refers to God, yet since all three are the one being of God, when you see one person of the Trinity, you always find the other two. Look up the following three passages from the Bible with this question in mind: Who raised Jesus from the dead?

John 2:19

Romans 8:11

Galatians 1:1

Three different verses, each giving a different person of the Trinity credit for the work of the resurrection. Indeed, it is not just the being of God that is one, but the action of God is unified as well! Embrace a better view of the threeness of God in which they are always one. And embrace a better view of the oneness of God in which it is always composed of the three. Always!

22 TIME AND ETERNITY IN JESUS

A model illustrating a Christo-centric view of time and eternity.

Let us see how Jesus can help illustrate time and eternity and get past the Arian problem. In the biblical story, time-space begins at creation with God's outpouring. At the end of the Book of Revelation, time-space is incorporated with eternity at the eschaton— the return of Christ and the universal restoration of creation.[89] The eschaton is when heaven and earth, time and eternity, and even God and humanity are brought together. What was separate is brought into communion with God through a final act of God's self-sacrificial love.

As previously discussed, eternity is that which transcends time. The classical view, wanting to protect God from the death and decay associated with passage or sequence, holds that God's eternity transcends not only time-space but also sequence itself (time in its narrowest sense). The Trinity forces us to revise the classical view in that God can experience sequence within the interpersonal communion of agape love that is the Trinity, that God seems to experience sequence with creation itself in human history, and especially in that Jesus lowered himself and entered human history as a human being.

Even so, the eternal God still transcends time-space, else God would be a part of creation rather than the Creator. So we can now represent time in a diagram, keeping in mind that we mean time in its fullest sense as history within time-space.

Time →

Figure 5.1: God, Eternity, and Time

---

[89] Acts 3:21, the "universal restoration."

A classical theist would represent time as finite (either a circle or a line), and eternity beyond would never touch it. An open theist, viewing time as simply sequence, would likely draw time and eternity together as one line of infinite time. In the Bible time begins (but does not end) with a more classical approach in which time is created and finite, with a beginning and end. Creation and eschaton represent this beginning and ending, which are boundary events—events in which time-space borders on the eternal. As Leslie Newbigin describes, these boundary events are events in which the laws of physics cease to apply.[90] They are beyond our ability to make rational sense of them, though they are revealed to us in Scripture. Below is a representation of time with these boundary events drawn in.

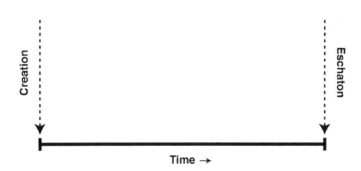

Figure 5.2: God, Eternity, and Time

We could replace the label "eschaton" with "restoration" or "sanctification" as understood in their ultimate sense. We cannot

---

[90] Leslie Newbigin, *The Gospel in a Pluralist Society* (Grand Rapids, MI: W.B. Eerdmans, 1989), 11.

speak to what is beyond these boundary events. They are beyond our comprehension and the scope of revelation given to us. Creation and eschaton are the brackets, or the envelope of time-space, as well as human comprehension, for there is no time, or any revelation given to us, beyond these boundaries. While God clearly exists beyond these parameters, and we will continue to exist in some way beyond (or upon) the eschaton, it will not be a time-bound existence as we know it. Eternity represents that which is outside of time-space, and can be added to the diagram by connecting the boundary events.

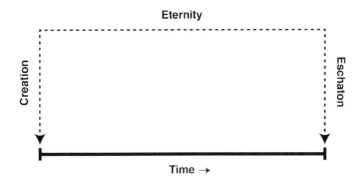

Figure 5.3: God, Eternity, and Time

Creation and eschaton are called boundary events because it is there that time and eternity come up against each other and interact in such a way as to condition all creation. The eternal God acts upon time-space with universal effect. No part of creation is exempt. Scripture describes the creation as the divine action that brings all time-space into existence, and it describes the eschaton as the divine action that brings all time-space to its ultimate consummation through integration with eternity.

At this point we have left out the crucial boundary event. It is the event of redemption (or atonement) in the person of Jesus Christ. This event takes place at a definitive point in historical time and space, through the historical Jesus, and is represented below with the label "Christ."

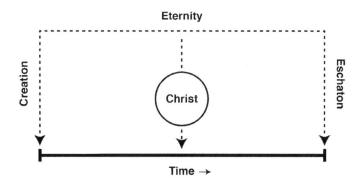

Figure 5.4: God, Eternity, and Time

Redemption in Jesus Christ is the central and pivotal boundary event. In Jesus, time and eternity do the inconceivable, coming together at the crux of the diagram.[91] Time-space comes into being at creation and consummates at the eschaton. In Jesus, eternity breaks into time-space and forms the crucial link between eternity and time. In this way, the person of Jesus, from his incarnation to his ascension, is the fulcrum boundary event. Jesus comes from beyond time, sent by the Father in the power of the Holy Spirit, yet he is

---

[91] When in historical time this happens does not matter as I am not meaning to imply that the life of Jesus happens historically exactly in the middle of created time between creation and eschaton.

born of a woman in the lineage and history of Israel. He then takes sin and death unto himself on the cross, and defeats them upon the resurrection. This is the fulcrum boundary because it is more than a boundary event; *it is a boundary-breaking event, and it is the only one of its kind, for it injects eternal life into time itself. The envelope of eternity around time is pierced clean through, the heavens are torn asunder, and God takes on the flesh of creation, bears the sin and death within it, and defeats it through agape love.*

How is it that time and eternity, being distinct by nature, can come together? The Son holds them together. In the person of Jesus, time and eternity cohere, not in that Jesus is between them, as with subordinationism, but in that he inhabits them both. This is what the Gospel teaches us. In Jesus the time-bound world of sickness gives way to God's healing. Likewise, in Jesus the grip of death is overcome by resurrection. The sin-laden world of shame gives way to forgiveness of sin and the inauguration of the new creation. Eternity literally breaks into the world in the person of Jesus. The Kingdom of God is at hand!

The Son in his dual nature, *while maintaining the distinctions* between them, *eliminates the separation* between God and humanity, between heaven and earth, and between eternity and time. As the Bible says, he is the way, the truth, and the life. That the eternal Son came in time has been argued to be the cause of needing an eternal Trinity and a temporal Trinity. The dual nature of Jesus makes dual trinities unnecessary when we are willing to accept Jesus at his word. The human, time-bound Jesus is also the eternal God, and that God in Jesus has chosen to reconcile the world to Godself.

To understand how Jesus coheres to eternity and time, I find it helpful to demonstrate how time moves forward, not only chronologically from creation to the eschaton, but also kairologically between these boundary events. In the Bible, *chronos* (or *kronos*) is the Greek word used for ordinary, chronological time. It is quantitative clock time or calendar time. Yet the Bible also uses the word *kairos* to describe God's time, the right time, or qualitative time. In the Gospel of Mark, Jesus begins his ministry by proclaiming, "The time [*kairos*] is fulfilled, and the Kingdom of God has come near; repent and believe in the good news."[92]

Kairos is God's eternity breaking into creation. We might experience moments in our lives when God seems to be breaking in, getting our attention, or intervening in some way. These can be thought of as "kairos moments,"[93] but a kairos moment is far different from the three boundary events of creation, Christ, and eschaton. This is because kairos moments can affect a particular time and place in creation—a mere moment in your life, albeit one that can have far reaching consequences. The three boundary events, however, are ultimate kairos events in that they condition *all* time and space. We can represent chronos and kairos on the model.

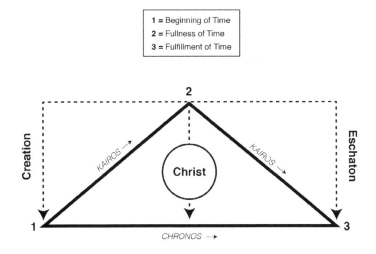

Figure 5.5: God, Eternity, and Time

The black triangle represents time moving forward in two senses,

---

[92] Mark 1:15

[93] Mike Breen and Steve Cockram, *Building a Discipling Culture* (Pawleys Island, SC: 3 Dimension Ministries, 2009), 26-40.

chronologically and kairologically. We live on the chronological line where time progresses chronologically in the successive pattern of historical events. Time also progresses kairologically toward what the biblical narrative describes as the divine purpose and the ultimate fulfillment of time. For first-century Palestinian Jews, the event of Jesus Christ was a chronological experience of time like any other. Yet Scripture tells us that this event was a kairological event like no other. Kairos is revealed to us and acts as a type of window into eternity, yet we can experience it only within our chronological frame.

The diagram does not denote that kairos is increasing from creation to Christ and decreasing from Christ to eschaton. Rather, it shows the direction and purpose of kairos as it moves to incorporate all things in Jesus (what I label the fullness of time). At the eschaton, all of creation can be incorporated into eternity (labeled the fulfillment of time). Time moves chronologically from creation to eschaton in the linear way we experience time, but time also borders eternity and moves kairologically from creation to its ultimate fullness in the person of Jesus Christ. At the event of Christ, eternity breaks into time-space, and inaugurates time-space's ultimate fulfillment, which will occur at the end of all things.

This is the narrative arc of the Bible, and we see it stated in Scripture:

> But when *the fullness of time* had come, God sent his Son, born of a woman, born under the law, in order to redeem those who were under the law.[94]

From the redemptive work of Christ, time-space then moves toward its ultimate fulfillment at the eschaton, where all things come together in unity under Christ. As Paul describes in Galatians:

> He made known to us the mystery of his will according to his good pleasure, which he purposed in Christ, to be put into effect when the *times reach their fulfillment*—to bring unity to all things in heaven and on earth under Christ.[95]

---

[94] Galatians 4:4–5 (emphasis mine)
[95] Ephesians 1:8–10 (NIV, emphasis mine)

As we'll see later, it is the entire Trinity at work, not just the Son, yet it is Jesus who is most immediate to us within time-space in the crucial boundary event. The first boundary event of creation is defined by the distinction of creation from God, while the last boundary event of eschaton is defined by incorporation of creation with God. The central boundary event of Christ is defined paradoxically by both distinction and incorporation simultaneously. Eternity and time, God and humanity, are still very much distinct. Yet they come together as one in the dual nature of Jesus. In Christ they remain distinguishable, yet become inseparable. Our eternal life in Jesus is bound to the paradox of his person.

| LIVE LIKE IT MATTERS |

They say that the past is gone and the future doesn't exist. True enough for us, but in Jesus nothing is wasted and nothing is lost (that doesn't want to be). The past and future exist for God in a way that is beyond human comprehension. Christ connects us to all that is, was, and will be. You are not stuck and not alone. Time and eternity are not so separate after all. So are you investing in eternal things? Do you even know what that would be? Relationships of sacrificial love are a good starting point. The love we pour out will not go to waste in God's economy, and in eternity we will see it overflow and fill us in return. Invest in one of those relationships today. It is only our fear of death and meaninglessness that is stopping us.

23 MARRIAGE AND MUTUAL SUBMISSION

Reciprocal submission in love is God's example and command to us.

The union between husband and wife is often compared to the Trinitarian communion. In the Creation story we are told that male and female are created in the image of God, implying that while they each uniquely reflect God, they better reflect God's image together, when they embody mutual submission in love. In Ephesians 5, Paul instructs wives to "submit to their husbands as to the Lord,"[96] and then uses different language for their culturally privileged husbands, telling them to "love your wives, just as Christ loved the Church and gave himself up for her."[97] Paul's main point, stated clearly in the first sentence of the paragraph, is obvious when we are able to see past our power struggles. He says to everyone, "Submit to one another out of reverence for Christ."[98]

God exists as a communion of mutual submission and empowerment, and God has redeemed the world in Christ through an act of submission that empowers us. Paul says in Ephesians that the way to revere Christ is to submit to one another. Apparently, submission is harder than it seems, or else Scripture wouldn't mention it at nearly every turn. It is true that we also see exhortations of non-mutual submission in Scripture (Colossians 3 is an example), especially to slaves and to wives. Yet in context these appear to be cultural accommodations for the sake of evangelism. When the culture glorifies non-mutual submission, we are called to submit in love anyway. We are commanded to love even when reciprocity is not expected. *The New Testament's instructions that we love one another, serve one another, and submit to one another form the central theme of how we are to respond to what God has done for us in Jesus.*

Love is so difficult because it is a sinless act that requires an active surrender. Surrender reflects the life of the Trinity, and to do so requires this life of God in us. Such love comprised the human

---

[96] Ephesians 5:22 (NIV)
[97] Ephesians 5:25 (NIV)
[98] Ephesians 5:21 (NIV)

experience before the fall, but the curse of sin has made lording over each other the norm. Upon the fall, God states to Eve the reality of sin: "Your desire will be for your husband, and he will rule over you."[99] Humanity's choice to not trust God and rule over ourselves resulted in our being contaminated by the drive to rule over each other. The rest of the Old Testament illustrates the deadly effects on the human community on an ever-larger scale, even as God intervenes time and time again to save his people. Jesus summed up the problem well, telling his disciples that the world is a system of "lording over each other."

Jesus commands us to no longer treat each other this way, but to serve one another. When his disciples argue among themselves for position and power he says,

> You know that the rulers of the Gentiles lord it over them, and their high officials exercise authority over them. Not so with you. Instead, whoever wants to become great among you must be your servant, and whoever wants to be first must be your slave—just as the Son of Man did not come to be served, but to serve, and to give his life as a ransom for many.[100]

If we seriously accept God's invitation to new life, then the curse of sin should no longer be the norm in our relationships. Mutual submission and service characterizes the divine relationship, and it should characterize any Christian relationship, especially marriage. What Jesus teaches his disciples in this passage is the same thing that Paul teaches the Ephesians. The disciples and the Ephesians wanted to know who among them was greatest, and the New Testament answer is consistent: You are greatest when you submit to and serve the other in love. Jesus says that the greatest must be the least. Paul instructs us, if we have any reverence for Jesus at all, to submit to one another. And to husbands, who in the cultural norms of the first

---

[99] Genesis 3:16 (NIV)
[100] Matthew 20:25–28

century had undisputed leadership and power in the eyes of the world, he ups the ante with the command to "love your wives, just as Christ loved the Church and gave himself up for her." Both passages are about leadership. *In God's Kingdom, service and leadership are one and the same.*

We will see in a later chapter that the egalitarian life of the Trinity does not imply sameness of persons, roles, or even power. Yet requiring submission from others without first submitting yourself to them with a heart to serve is a failure to lead. It is how the world works when it rejects God's invitation, resulting in the sin that breaks relationship. It is to choose death over life, hell over heaven. Any rejection of mutual submission is a rejection of the Trinity who exists in and through it, and is a rejection of Jesus, who shows us perfect love through sacrifice and service. To choose Jesus is to choose a better way—*The Way*. In becoming a true communion of equals who mutually submit, husband and wife participate in the life of God that sustains creation. In a marriage of love, the Trinity looks down and sees a clearer image.

| LIVE LIKE IT MATTERS |

Mutual submission is easier said than done. It is much easier to be either passive (a false type of submission), or aggressive and domineering. While there are plenty of the domineering type, I find that most people go the passive, or passive aggressive route. You see it in many marriages. The distant, cynical, or distracted spouse is all too common.

There is nothing passive about the mutual submission among Father, Son, and Holy Spirit. Submission in love is an act that empowers and brings life. And neither do they wait for someone else to go first. In a sense, each of them is always going first, and that should characterize our relationships, especially our marriages. So how can you go first in your marriage or other significant relationship? Don't keep reading until the answer comes to you!

24 THEOLOGICAL DILEMMAS

How to honestly have it both ways.

I'm not someone who likes to live with contradictions. Mystery and paradox shouldn't be thrown around lightly, for they can be used to obscure an issue and discourage genuine solutions. Yet to accept Jesus is to accept the paradox he reveals. He is fully God and fully human. Also, God is three persons and one being. This cross-paradox forms a foundation on which we can inform our theological problems. It is a fantastical foundation, yet through the faith of Jesus, and subsequently through our faith in Jesus, the fantastic is shown to be real. The upside of a Christo-centric view is that starting from Christ's paradox does not result in a faith with ever-multiplying dualities and contradictions. Rather, we can readily resolve them using the paradoxical Jesus.

The dual nature of Jesus holds time and eternity together. It is as Paul states in Colossians 1:15–20, "The Son is the image of the invisible God. . . . He is before all things, and in him all things hold together. . . . For God was pleased to have all his fullness dwell in him." If we accept the Jesus and Trinity paradoxes, we can conclude that God is both within and beyond time. Yet while our encounter with the divine is a genuine encounter with the eternal God, it is not the totality of the eternal God. *God limits himself on our behalf so that what is finite can have a finite glimpse of the infinite.* Eternity and time-space remain distinct and, by nature, separate categories, at least until they are brought together at the eschaton, yet even now they are held together as one in Christ, who himself exists fully in both, and who even now by his Spirit—the Holy Spirit—genuinely dwells among us.

We cannot collapse Jesus' human and divine natures into one, making Jesus a demi-God. Yet neither can we separate one nature from the other, making him two persons. They exist perfectly together without annihilating each other or fusing to become a hybrid. It is what Western theologians call the hypostatic union. A Christian from China once explained to me that the yin-yang symbol was helpful to him in visualizing the principle of Jesus' two natures being distinguishable yet inseparable. However you visualize paradox, faith in Jesus requires an embrace of it.

The Father has from eternity (from beyond time) sent the Son, and from eternity the Son has humbled himself. Through God's free choice to love us, Jesus' humanity became inseparable, yet always distinguishable, from his divinity. This allows us to have it both ways on some sticky theological issues where there are traditional splits and a disintegrated understanding. The divide generally has to do with our ideas of divine/eternal considerations vs. human/temporal considerations:

God Beyond Time (Eternal Trinity)	*vs.*	God Within Time (Temporal Trinity)
Divine Jesus	*vs.*	Human Jesus
God's Being	*vs.*	God's Becoming
God's Foreknowledge	*vs.*	Human Free Will
God's Separation From Us	*vs.*	God's Presence With Us

Figure 6: Disintegrated Theology

These two poles prioritize God as either eternal or temporal. The classical tradition has prioritized the eternal, thinking to find God's being outside of time. The problem here is that, since we are temporal beings, we can not accurately know anything about an eternal God, or experience this God who is beyond creation. It is only through God's revelation, given to us within time, and most perfectly in Jesus Christ, that we can know or experience God. The problem with this counter-argument is that God must also transcend created time-space for him to be the Creator of it. It is simply the left and right sides of the table above.

Jesus, who is fully in time and fully in eternity, can inform solutions to the paradoxes we see in the Bible, such as free will and determinism. Rather than each side arguing that half of the scriptural texts on the subject are wrong, I propose that we use the person of Jesus to inform a solution. His dual nature in time implies free will, as a time-bound, human perspective cannot know the future, while his dual nature in eternity implies determinism, or at least foreknowledge, as an eternal perspective knows all things. The two exist paradoxically together in Christ.

The classical notion of a God with an absolute view above all of time is incomplete, as is the opposing view in which God's view is only within time. The boundary-breaking event of Christ unites God's absolute position beyond time with his particular position within time. Christ paradoxically maintains the distinction while eliminating the separation. Just as Jesus' two natures are perfectly united without annihilating each other, his two positions within and beyond time are perfectly united without one annihilating the other.

One side argues that God is not free if he is not independent of creation with total foreknowledge. The other argues that God's choices cannot be free if God has foreknowledge of how he will act towards us in the future. Love cuts through such philosophical dualities. Whether God knows or not becomes a moot point—God will always do the most loving thing! And God already knows that the most loving thing is exactly what he will do in every circumstance! It is simply who he is as God. For love to be love, it must be freely given and received, not predetermined. Yet for love to be love, one must be predetermined to do all that love requires. One side of the coin does not annihilate the other. Paradoxically, they inform and define each other.

Holding both ends of the spectrum at once is difficult, yet since we can integrate the eternal and temporal trinities through the dual nature of the Son, we are now free, and perhaps even obliged, to have it both ways on the issues that derive from them. That Jesus is fully God and fully human is the root paradox of the faith, and it seems to be the root of contention in each issue listed on Figure 6. Once we simultaneously accept the nature of the Son as well as the further paradox of Trinity, then we can conclude that the Trinity is itself both within and beyond time, for the Trinity is one being and not three. If we can hold that tension and resist the urge to release it by subordinating Jesus, then we arrive at a point where holding two perspectives on the temporal-eternal spectrum is the natural position. I think of this as an integrated understanding:

God Beyond Time (Eternal Trinity) *and* God Within Time (Temporal Trinity)
Divine Jesus *and* Human Jesus
God's Being *and* God's Becoming
God's Foreknowledge *and* Human Free Will
God's Separation From Us *and* God's Presence With Us

Figure 7: Integrated Theology

Figure 7 shows us that there is unity with distinction, much like the Trinity being three persons and one being. In my opinion it is not unlike the paradox we have in physics between general relativity and quantum mechanics. Both have been borne out as fully and empirically true, yet they were each themselves fantastical when first proposed, and they contradict each other despite the herculean efforts by thousands of the smartest scientists to unite them. Each indicates that the other must be false, yet both are true. Likewise, if God is within as well as beyond time-space, then we can easily have it both ways, and I believe that the paradoxical nature of Scripture on this topic demands we do.

Using spatial dimensions is a way of imagining how two opposing truths can exist together in Jesus. Beings living in a plane of two spatial dimensions would experience only length and width. If we were to pierce their world with a three-dimensional cone-shaped object, then they would perceive it only as a flat shape. If the cone went through their plane point-first (straight up or down), then the two-dimensional beings would see a perfect circle, which would expand or shrink as we moved the cone through the plane. Yet if the cone went through on its side, then it would appear as a perfect triangle that would either grow or shrink as we moved it through the plane.[101] There would simply be no way for two-dimensional beings to experience that the triangle and the circle were in fact the same thing—the exact same thing. In fact, to them this would seem contradictory and quite impossible. With God's eternity breaking into time, I believe that something similar is happening, which is how free will and God's foreknowledge may be "flat" ways of looking at the same "extra dimensional" thing. The circle and the triangle *contradict each other* at one level, but on a higher level, as with the example of the cone, *they actually define each other as one entity.*

Here is another way to think about it: Physical space on earth is defined by boundaries, yet these boundaries are defined by space. Space and boundaries are not the same thing—they contradict at one level, but at a higher level we can understand that they come together as one entity. God's eternal perspective need not negate human freedom, and God's temporal perspective need not negate divine freedom and sovereignty. I propose that one defines the other, and vice versa—as with the cone being experienced as either a circle or a triangle, and never both, from the perspective of lesser-dimensional beings. When we hold the dual nature of Jesus and the relational nature of the egalitarian Trinity simultaneously, there is no need to preserve the "either-or" of these theological dilemmas. God literally worked it out in the person of Jesus.

Advances in the biological and neurological sciences are indicating that everything about us and our decisions are predetermined by our circumstances and biology. Yet advances in physics and quantum mechanics are indicating the opposite—that everything at a fundamental level is not predetermined but decided randomly within a field of relational probabilities. Which is true?

---

[101] Ross, *Beyond the Cosmos.* I've heard this idea in many contexts, but have seen this particular example here. Ross's book focuses on theological applications of multidimensional possibilities.

How about general relativity vs. quantum theory? Circle or triangle? God's foreknowledge or free will? Love entails free will and predeterminism together. It is the circle and triangle working together to make a cone. Love, God's interpersonal being itself, is a higher reality, even as it holds us, in our lower dimension, together in relationship.

| LIVE LIKE IT MATTERS |

Perhaps the best way to live out this chapter practically is to cultivate a peace of mind around these theological dilemmas. You may be someone who geeks out over them, perhaps championing one side or another. Or maybe you are someone who willfully ignores them or thinks that you are not smart enough to understand them (which might be true for everybody). They are only worth thinking about if they help to give us the peace of God. Arguing or worrying won't accomplish that.

If we can accept that Jesus is who the Bible says he is, then his paradoxical nature becomes a lens through which the paradox of these theological issues becomes unified. Instead of contradicting each other, the two sides of each issue begin to complement and inform each other, demonstrating greater dimensionality. In Jesus the richness of the Bible and the amazing mysteries of God become more profound and practical at the same time. So stop arguing, and stop ignoring, and start accepting. You can't force acceptance upon yourself, but the more you practice being a little uncomfortable, resting simply with what is, the closer you will come.

25 JESUS IS LORD OF ALL

How the Son makes Christianity universally true.

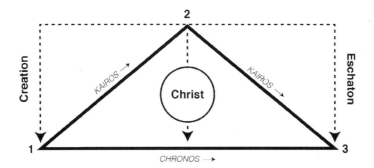

In the picture above, *Figure 5.5: God, Eternity, and Time*, see how at the particular historical moment of Jesus Christ, eternity and time come together at a single point: At the top of the triangle, kairos completes its upward sweep toward eternity. At that point in time, eternity breaks into time as Christ enters creation. In this way all of time is now connected to eternity in Jesus Christ. Eternity is collapsed into the fullness of kairos, even as it breaks into chronos at a unique historical point—the historical life of Jesus. Jesus does not *just* exist as a particular human at a particular time and place. Neither does he *just* exist outside of time in eternity. Time and eternity hold together in him. The event of Christ compresses eternity into a single point that breaks into creation. The result is a radical reconditioning of time-space. This is the Good News—metaphysically speaking.

The eternal envelope is pierced right through, allowing eternity to not only enter time, but to inaugurate the taking up of time into eternity itself. We see glimpses of this in Christ's birth, in which the eternal God becomes a helpless baby; in Christ's baptism, in which Mark tells us that the heavens were "torn apart";[102] and of course in the cosmic events of Christ's death and resurrection. Eternity breaks into a historical point in time-space in the person of Jesus, revealing that Jesus is within creation while still being one with the divine communion beyond it. In Jesus is our salvation and the promise of the eschaton—not just theologically, but literally in his person!

In this way Jesus Christ is "the way, the truth, and the life"[103] for all time and through all eternity. This is why Scripture speaks of the redemptive work of Jesus as "the eternal covenant."[104] Chronologically it is rightly referred to as the "new covenant," but kairologically it is not new; it is the eternal covenant, making it true for all people—within, throughout, and beyond time. Being a boundary event like creation and eschaton, redemption in Christ effects time-space universally, making the Gospel more than a story, and more even than history—it is universal history.[105] As Paul writes in Colossians, "For in [Jesus], the fullness of God was pleased to dwell, and through him God was pleased to reconcile to himself all things, whether on earth or in heaven, by making peace through the blood of his cross."[106] The invitation to life in Jesus is true for everyone. Of course, people are free to decline the invitation.

God desires relationship with all of us, regardless of our sex and gender identity, our status, race, and culture, where we live, and even when we live. What makes Christianity so wonderful and simultaneously so offensive is this universal claim: Jesus—the particular, historical, human Jesus—eliminates the divide between eternity and time, and between God and humanity. This particular person who lived in a particular place is not only God, but also is the key to understanding who God is as well as the way to God for all

---

[102] Mark 1:10
[103] John 14:16
[104] Hebrews 13:20-21
[105] Newbigin, *The Gospel in a Pluralist Society*, 89.
[106] Colossians 1:19–20

humanity, for all time. This is the "scandal of particularity."[107] It seems exclusive, unfair even. Why was he not born someone or somewhere or sometime else? Jesus is just so . . . well, particular!

That Jesus would come as a man and not a woman is particularly scandalous (just as it would be the other way around). That Jesus would come in the first century and not the 21st is a scandal. That Jesus was a Palestinian Jew and not Chinese or English or Zulu or Cherokee is a scandal. That God incarnate would be revealed in the flesh to a few in one place and time and not to all is a scandal. That the events of the Bible take place in genocidal, patriarchal, and slave-owning times and places is scandalous.

Yet to get caught up in these scandals is to miss the point. *All of human history is scandalous, but Christianity's claim is that God is a God who acts in our history and, through Jesus, dwells in it in order to redeem it.* God, in the person of Jesus Christ, who is sent by the Father in the power of the Holy Spirit, has from eternity broken into our world in the flesh. God has done this not to validate the various particularities that separate us from God and each other—things such as time, place, culture, sex, genocide, patriarchy, slavery, and all aspects of broken relationship caused by the effects of sin[108]—but to overcome them all. He even overcame the ultimate separation, death itself.

In Jesus, God has humbled himself once and for all in order to raise us up into eternal communion, bringing heaven and earth together in a very real, if not yet fully realized way. This is certainly a radical Christianizing of our understanding of God and the world. And to risk an understatement, this is good news! This allows us to have a higher view of Jesus that elevates his divinity and humanity at the same time. It also allow us to have an understanding of the Trinity that is the same for both the eternal and the temporal trinities. And finally, it shows us how Jesus is universally true for all people throughout time and space.

---

[107] Newbigin, *The Gospel in a Pluralist Society*, 72.

[108] Of course, not all of these things are bad (aspects and differences between sexes, cultures, etc. are to be celebrated as God given), but in a fallen world they can bring about further alienation.

| LIVE LIKE IT MATTERS |

In Jesus, God and humanity, heaven and earth, time-space and eternity, come together. Yet for us, these barriers still exist, even as they are paradoxically eliminated in Christ. Eternal life starts here and now. Yet before we can experience the life of the resurrection at the end of the story, we first have to walk through the beginning of the story. We cannot follow Jesus into his resurrected life without first following him in his human suffering and death. So as we each face our own death, take heart, Jesus has overcome the world![109]

There is a reality higher than your oppression, mistreatment, and difficulties. This reality is greater even than death. Trusting in this reality means living a life with less worry and more compassion for the problems of others. Start today! Give your burdens over to God in prayer and ask for his larger perspective. Let's grow together toward an eternal view. Make a list of your burdens. Write them all down and pray. Give them to the Lord. He already holds them. We just need to let go.

---

[109] John 16:33

PART III

HOW AND WHY MATTERS

26 GOD IS OTHER-CENTERED

Bearing the imago Dei is a communal, other-centered activity.

Other-centeredness is intrinsic to the Trinity. Each person gives his life over to the others, empowering the others. In doing so, each is in turn filled and enlivened by the others.[110] This is the beauty of perichoresis. Paradoxically, each divine person empties himself, even as he transcends himself, even as he becomes his fullest self. God is selfless and self-full in this way, and we are invited to be the same. As Jesus demonstrated, if we are going to find our life, we are going to have to pour our lives out for others.

Sadly, the Church in the West has lost this image, and is only now recovering it. Many have settled for a version of the self-centered God of Greek philosophy. This God is what classical philosophy calls "absolute," which in essence means *unrelated.* The ancient Greek school of thought taught that the being of God was an absolute substance—which is where we get the language of the Trinity as one being or "substance". In the fifth century, the neo-platonist minded St. Augustine used psychological analogies to explain the Trinity in a new way. His desire was to combat subordinationism by focusing on the one substance of God. His analogies portrayed God not so much as one being in three persons, but more as one person with three aspects. Our experience of ourselves as subject, object, and the love (or predicate) between them were, in Augustine's view, vestiges of the Trinity and proof that humanity was made in God's image.

Thinking of the Father, Son, and Holy Spirit as aspects of a single subjectivity has dominated the West ever since—the Father as eternal subject, the Son as the eternal object, and the Spirit as the bond of love between them. There isn't anything wrong with Augustine's analogies, but Western society has emphasized them so much that we have had trouble seeing that God is a community of inter-subjective persons, and we tend to view God in either subordinationist or modalist ways. Eastern Christianity struggles with subordinationism

---

[110] Colin E. Gunton, *The Promise of Trinitarian Theology* (New York, NY: T&T Clark Ltd, 2006), 10.

as well, but in its own way. While the East has always started with the three, there is an ambivalence in the East having to do with the *Monarche*—the "one source" of God from whom all things are derived. Some view the *Monarche* as the Father to the exclusion of Son and Spirit, while others view it as the Trinity.

Here in the West, what Augustine began, others would promote and perfect over the centuries. God's individual subjectivity became the essence of God. Descartes' famous statement—I think therefore I am—would not have been possible without Augustine. In fact, nearly all of modern philosophy and psychology in the West harkens back to Augustine's idea of God's subjectivity. Over time, God as the absolute substance gave way to God as the absolute subject. God's subjectivity still had to be protected from relationship with fallen creation, just as the Greeks desired to protect the absolute substance.[111] In other words, God had to be an unrelated individual.

For centuries, our individual subjectivity has been held up as the closest thing we have to God. From this, we've inherited our culture of individualism with all of its benefits and drawbacks. The problem is that individual subjectivity is always *my* subjectivity. It cannot be yours or ours. Augustine moved us in the right direction with subjectivity, but what we have forgotten is that God is inter-subjective and inter-related. God is a community of persons, not just a person with his own inner-relations. Our faith is in a communal God, but this communion has not always informed our practice.

Rather than bearing the relational image of God, we have made God in our own self image. In our self-centered world in which we mirror our self-made God, people do what's best for them. My perspective matters most. My interests should be represented by my vote and my government. We can all feel good about this individual ethos, but it inevitably aids the powerful and harms the weak. Those with the most power always win over the disadvantaged. Hierarchies are promoted and maintained. Empathy and action for others comes

---

[111] Jürgen Moltmann, "The Fellowship of the Holy Spirit," *The Fellowship of the Holy Spirit—Trinitarian Pneumatology* 37, no. 3 (1984): 288–89. Moltmann describes how the ontologies of both substance and subject have undermined the Trinity.

secondary, and only when savvy marketers make them about how it makes *me* feel. Love is lost. Thus the Church often fails to love those who are different, causing us to lose our witness and forfeit our mission in the world.

To be created in the image of God is to be created not only in the image of the one, but also the three, as God is one being in three persons. Neither the one nor the three comes before the other. When we see image bearing as a solo sport, we become less able to see God in other people, other communities, and in the relationships among people. We forget about the other-centered love that is God, and that makes us who we are. We lose ourselves, even as we try to gain the world.

All things exist as an act of communion—that is, of persons in relationship. That God exists as Trinity implies that communion is the ground of being for all creation.[112] It is our relationships that make us the individuals that we are. All things exist as a function of their relation to God and subsequently to other things. From subatomic particles and the fundamental forces of the universe (may the forces be with you ☺),[113] which are themselves relational interactions, to human families and societies, relationships make and define us. Nothing exists apart from relationship, and through it we are created, redeemed, and sanctified. All being is relational. All meaning is social. All love is personal.

While you uniquely bear God's image, you do not do so alone. Godly relationship expresses the unity in diversity that we see in the Trinity. Together is how we bear God's image. We must teach a better vision of God as community in our churches. We must preach on who we are as communal image bearers. We must look at those who are different from us and ask two questions:

How do they uniquely bear the image of God?

How can we bear the image of God together?

As people created in the image of the triune God, we were made

---

[112] Zizioulas, *Being as Communion: Studies in Personhood and the Church*, 17.

[113] The four accepted fundamental interactions in the universe are the gravitational, electromagnetic, strong nuclear, and weak nuclear forces.

for relationship. Everything rests on the mutual, self-giving love of the Trinity. It is the stuff of life. And since divine relationship is a community of equals who submit in freedom to each other, then that is a clue bigger than the universe that the ideal human relationship is similarly egalitarian.

| LIVE LIKE IT MATTERS |

God is a community of persons who find their personhood through surrendering their lives to each other. They lose their lives to find them. Jesus said that we should do the same if we want to find our own life. This does not mean that you meet every human need around you, for nobody can do that. It means that you find a calling that gives life to others, and you pour your life into that. It could be your job, or more likely something outside of your job, like a hobby, ministry, or organization. Even family counts, though our calling usually goes beyond our immediate family.

Frederick Buechner famously said that "The place God calls you is the place where your deep gladness and the world's deep hunger meet." The world's hunger is everywhere, so all you have to figure out is: What is your deep gladness? Making coffee? Raising children? Negotiating business deals? Helping others grow in faith? What inspires you to pour out your life for others? You are not alone if you don't know, but it is worth taking some time, even a few years, to find out! Pray about it, talk to mentors about it, and most importantly, try things! Now God may daily call you to things that are not your deep gladness. Sacrifice is a part of giving and receiving life, and of being a follower of Jesus. Yet you don't have to do it all, as you do not bear God's image alone.

27 THE MODEL OF THE ACTUAL TRINITY

A dynamic, multi-directional perichoresis that incorporates the economy of salvation.

The model below imagines the Trinity holistically. If you are into theology, then I recommend you read Appendices 1 and 2 before reading this section, as they explore other models and their limitations, as well as the hazards of any integrative model. In presenting an integrative and egalitarian model of the Trinity, I would emphasize that the model is *descriptive*, not *prescriptive*, of the life of the Trinity. That is, it gives us a picture that makes sense of our experience and the biblical witness rather than giving definitive rules.

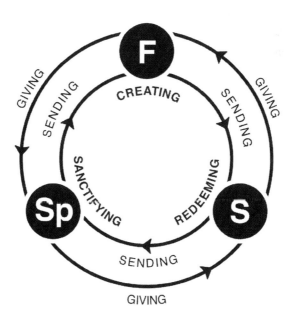

Figure 8: The Trinity—Integrated, Egalitarian, and Dynamic

In this egalitarian and integrative model, each of the three divine persons "empties," or pours himself out, into the other two persons simultaneously. Both directions are kenotic in that God gives Godself to Godself in such a way that the action of each divine person always empowers the other two. It is the extension or overflow of this same eternal kenosis that is our experience of God on behalf of the world in the economy of salvation. I have labeled the two kenotic movements "sending" and "giving." Each divine person empties into the others by the sending of one and by the giving of power and authority over that sending to the other.

By "sending" I mean the movement of God as actively initiated by one divine person, and then actively performed in perfect submission by another. By "giving" I mean the active submission, or yielding of divine authority, by one divine person and the subsequent use of that authority by another. The sending and giving go together. Each person does them both simultaneously. For example, as we see in the Gospels: The Father, for the world's redemption, sends the Son, who lives into the sending in submission to the Father. Simultaneously the Father gives authority to the Holy Spirit to actively govern redemption and empower the Son who is sent. Allow me to describe the entire illustration:

The Holy Spirit empties into both the Father and the Son simultaneously. For the purposes of creation by the Father, the Holy Spirit pours himself out bidirectionally—in the sending of the Father for creation and in giving his divine authority over creation to the Son. The Spirit sends the Father in the power of the Son. In creation the Father is the central actor whom we experience as immediate to us. Yet our experience of the Father in creation is the self-emptying of the Holy Spirit in the power of the Son. It is an experience of the Trinity who is both within and beyond time.

The Father empties into both the Son and the Holy Spirit simultaneously. For the purposes of redemption in the person of Jesus Christ, the Father pours himself out bidirectionally—in the sending of the Son to earth as humanity incarnate, and in giving his divine authority over redemption to the Holy Spirit. The Father sends the Son in the power of the Holy Spirit. In redemption the Son is the central actor whom we experience as immediate to us. Yet our experience of the Son is the self-emptying of the Father in the power of the Spirit. It is an experience of the Trinity who is both within and beyond time.

The Son empties into both the Holy Spirit and the Father simultaneously. For the purposes of sanctification by the Spirit, the Son pours himself out bidirectionally—in the sending of the Holy Spirit for sanctification and in giving his divine authority over sanctification to the Father. The Son sends the Spirit in the divine power of the Father. In sanctification the Spirit is the central actor whom we experience as immediate to us. Yet our experience of the Spirit is the self-emptying of the Son in the power of the Father. It is an experience of the Trinity who is both within and beyond time.

This perichoresis of the Trinity is an undivided whole, and it is seen temporally in three acts that consecutively platform each person of the Trinity. In the process, each successively acts upon the world. One person is the immediate actor to us, yet in one we always see the other two, for they are one in being and one in action. Whenever we experience one person of the Trinity, we always experience the other two in and through him.

The model could be said to be a social model of the Trinity, but it avoids the tritheistic danger of what Gunton refers to with social analogies of the Trinity that lack the perichoresis:

> One danger of the concept of communion—and especially of a "social" analogy of the Trinity—is of a form of tritheism which appears to relate the three persons in such a way as to suggest that they have distinct wills. Here lies the importance of the doctrine of the *perichoresis*, the inter-animation in relation, of Father, Son, and Spirit that is such that all that is done is indeed the act of all three.[114]

The model is profoundly perichoretic, moving in two directions at once. And not only in two directions, but also in the two "realms" of eternity and time, in and for Godself as well as in and for the

---

[114] Gunton, *The Promise of Trinitarian Theology*, 198.

world. It is perfect egalitarian kenosis in which both directions of divine self-emptying are active. Yet the activity of each divine person is completely dependent upon the other two, demonstrating the perfect unity of God's being. This allows us to also avoid the modalism so entrenched within Western Christianity. As Jürgen Moltmann explains:

> In their perichoresis and because of it, the Trinitarian persons are not to be understood as three different individuals, who only subsequently enter into relationship with one another (which is the customary reproach, under the name of "tritheism"). But they are not, either, three modes of being or three repetitions of the One God, as the modalistic interpretation suggests. The doctrine of the perichoresis links together in a brilliant way the threeness and the unity, without reducing the threeness to the unity, or dissolving the unity in the threeness.[115]

In one person the other two are always revealed. This is how we have perfect access to the Son even though Jesus has ascended to the right hand of the Father—because the person of the Holy Spirit universally represents Jesus to all people for all time.[116] Through relationship with the Son, we have relationship with the Father, and through relationship with the Holy Spirit, we have relationship with the Son. As Jesus testifies to what he hears from the Father,[117] so the Holy Spirit testifies to what he hears from the Son.[118] The Trinity is three persons, yet the Trinity is one being, and that being is characterized by the love that Father, Son, and Spirit have in and for each other, and lovingly extend to us.

"No one has greater love than this, to lay down one's life for one's friends."[119] In Jesus we find the perfect love of God, whose

---

[115] Jürgen Moltmann, *The Trinity and the Kingdom: The Doctrine of God*, Fortress Press ed. (Minneapolis, MN: Fortress Press, 1993), 175.

[116] Daniel Migliore, *Faith Seeking Understanding: An Introduction to Christian Theology* (Grand Rapids, MI: Eerdman's, 2004), 226–28.

[117] John 12:44–50, 14:10

[118] John 14:25–26, 15:26, 16:12–15

[119] John 15:13

example we are to follow. "We know love by this, that [Jesus] laid down his life for us, and we ought to lay our lives down for one another."[120] Clearly Jesus laid down his life in love for us, yet this love is the overflow of the love he has for the Father and the Holy Spirit. In reference to his upcoming death in the same passage in John, Jesus says, "I do as the Father has commanded me, so that the world may know that I love the Father."[121] The idea of dying was not something Jesus had on his own, for in his human condition he had to learn obedience by submitting to the will of the Father.[122] Neither was the idea of dying simply dictated to Jesus by the Father from eternity, for the Trinity is of one perfect will. From eternity the three divine persons willed together in perfect love how to save humanity; they would eternally join themselves to humanity in the person of Jesus Christ.

We have now incorporated the biblical movement of revelation within the model of the actual Trinity: creation to redemption to restoration, and with it the new creation. Bringing the work of the Trinity in time-space together with the eternal dance of the Trinity results in a thoroughly integrative model, and we have avoided the four hazards of integration (see appendix 1: subordinationism, static egalitarianism, pantheism, and not integrating to protect God's freedom). The God in human history and the God who exists in eternal divine communion are one and the same, and not just in theory, but in practice! We have no need for separate trinities. More provocatively, we have boldly removed the classical asymmetry of the Father as absolute God to the exclusion of the Son and the Holy Spirit.

In the act of redemption, the Son submits to the will of the Father and is dependent upon the Holy Spirit. In the act of sanctification, the Holy Spirit submits to the will of the Son and is dependent upon the Father. In the act of creation, the Father submits to the will of the Holy Spirit and is dependent upon the Son through

---

[120] 1 John 3:16
[121] John 14:31
[122] Hebrews 5:8

whom all things were created. God is unchanging in that the Trinity is always who God is, but that communion is a dynamic relationality, always in the motion of reciprocal love. The Father, Son, and Holy Spirit continually empty themselves into each other even as they are filled by each other. They pour out their life on behalf of each other, and they have chosen to extend that life to the world.

God exists as an act of communion in which the very being of God is found in the Trinity rather than in the Father alone. The Father does not precede the communion, for he, like the Son and Holy Spirit, exists by it, in it, and through it. There is no Father without the Son and Spirit, and there never has been. The submission of the Son to the Father can now be seen in its larger context. It is not eternal subordination; it is simply part of the mutual, dynamic submission of the Trinity. *The Son indeed submits to the Father eternally, and so, too, the Holy Spirit and the Father submit eternally. It is constitutive of their triune being.*

The Son's submission to the Father as seen in the Gospels is a snapshot, if you will, of the divine communion. It is a still frame captured during the earthly ministry of Jesus, when he was completely dependent upon the Holy Spirit and completely submitted to the Father. A snapshot taken during creation or restoration would yield a different picture as the Trinitarian persons work together in the creation, redemption, and sanctification of the world. Yet while the picture of who is submitting or sending might change, the picture is always one of dynamic, mutual submission

Granted, the clearest snapshot that we have is the snapshot of the incarnated Son in our redemption. Our picture of creation and sanctification is much more obscure, but we see enough in Scripture to see that these are also extensions of the divine perichoresis. We will see in a further chapter how this model is well-represented by the biblical witness. While the eternal picture may be veiled to us, we can assume that it is accurately characterized by the temporal picture, in which one divine person sends a second and relinquishes power and authority to the third.

While I did not illustrate it as part of Figure 8, the world (or all time-space) can be envisioned in the center of the model of the actual Trinity, in which the eternal perichoresis of God overflows to and includes the world in creation, redemption, and sanctification. If we did represent time in the model, we could imagine it beginning within the inner circle at creation/creating, where it would spiral around and outward, being consummated at the eschaton after completing one spiral rotation.

We can imagine *Figure 5.5: God, time, and eternity,* being reshaped and curved so that God's perichoresis surrounds the spiral of time, as opposed to time simply moving from left to right in the linear way Western religions conceive of it. Yet this is not the repetitive, circular view of time promoted by the Eastern religions either. Time is moving towards something, but not a cliff or an endless infinity (time as a line) nor its own repetition (time as a circle), but a new beginning as promised by Scripture (time as a spiral) with a new heaven and a new earth.

| LIVE LIKE IT MATTERS |

Perichoresis is usually pictured as flowing in one direction, but I believe it goes both ways. We too are meant to be poured into by more than one person, even as we pour into multiple people. Like God, we should be giving away our power and our mission, sending and empowering others. And we must be open to others sending and empowering us. So whom can you empower today? What authority can you entrust to another, allowing the love and mission of God to expand? Don't hoard it all to yourself. Let the water flow out and then be refreshed by new, living water. It is the way of God.

28 AGAPE AND HIERARCHY

Mutual submission is not identical relations.

The Trinity would not exist, nor would anything else, without the agape-love of God, "for God is agape."[123] Mutual submission is intrinsic to God's agape. Each divine person empties and fills each other, as they selflessly indwell each other, while being/becoming their fullest selves. Mutual submission is dynamically symmetrical—persons take on unique roles with real power differentials in order to accomplish something in love. In this mutuality there are not permanent levels of uneven worth or power. It is this dynamic symmetry that Jesus expects of his followers, as he declares to his disciples, "You know that the rulers of the Gentiles lord it over them, and their high officials exercise authority over them. Not so with you. Instead, whoever wants to become great among you must be your servant."[124]

In agape, servanthood and leadership are reciprocal and united in that God demonstrates leadership not only through power but also through service. "Therefore be imitators of God, as beloved children, and live in love, as Christ loved us and gave himself up for us, a fragrant offering and sacrifice to God."[125] The example of Jesus then becomes our model of mutual submission. We are to "be subject to one another out of reverence for Christ."[126] For God, self-sacrifice is the greatest form of love and power. As God said to Paul, "My power is made perfect in weakness."[127] God's ultimate display of servile weakness on the cross contained enough power to redeem the entire cosmos.

The subordinationist view of the nature of our relationship with the Trinity sees God in a hierarchical way. In this thinking, the Father is above the Son, who in turn is above or perhaps equal to the Holy

---

[123] 1 John 4:8
[124] Matthew 20:25-27 (NIV). See also Mark 10:42–45 and Luke 22:25–27.
[125] Ephesians 5:1–2
[126] Ephesians 5:21
[127] 2 Corinthians 12:9

Spirit. The Holy Spirit brings us into relationship with the Son, who in turn brings us into relationship with the Father. Now we certainly do see in the Bible that we come into relationship with God in this way, but when we begin to understand the sequence of those relationships as corresponding to levels of divinity, then our view is subordinationist, and we start to think like Arians.

While most who assume a hierarchical view may not make the connection, the view promotes belief in the Father as absolute God to the exclusion of the Son and Spirit. The Son and Spirit function only to bring us into some sort of right transactional arrangement with the Father; they are good for little else. Relationship with the Son and Spirit is not important in and of itself. The Son and Spirit are "a sufficiently watered-down form of deity to engage, and even to enter, the visible, created order." This is what Richard Norris calls "semi-Arianism."[128] The divinity of the Son and the Holy Spirit are reduced, along with our relationship with God.

This approach throws away the Trinity. With it, God does not exist as act of communion at all, for God is the Father alone, from whom the Trinity is derived. And this Godless religion excludes all possibility of a real or a direct relationship between God and humanity. Here the Gospel is drawn in a way that denies the power of what divine love is, for the self-giving love of God is no longer the giving of Godself to Godself and to the world, but rather the animating of demigods (Son and Spirit) to run connections between God and the world. It is simply a version of ancient Greek mythology and Greek philosophy with Christian vocabulary substituted in, which is perhaps exactly what the Arians and even the Gnostics had in mind.

And here we arrive at the crux of the problem: for we do come to Jesus through the Holy Spirit, and we do come to the Father through the Son. Jesus does submit to the Father and to the Holy Spirit. It is not the characteristics of submission and dependence that are unbiblical, it is the subordination that results from having too small a

---

[128] Richard Norris, "Trinity," in *The Holy Spirit: Classic and Contemporary Readings*, ed. Eugene F. Rogers (Chichester, West Sussex, UK: Wiley-Blackwell, 2009), 35.

view of the Trinity when we fail to integrate the eternal and temporal trinities through the dual nature of the Son. When we see the larger picture of the Trinitarian relations as dynamic and mutual, then they can be seen as part of the divine perichoresis—the agape love of God.

It is not the Father alone who is the source of divinity. We do not climb up any hierarchical or gnostic ladder in our approach to God. Real relationship with God is extended to us here and now in Jesus through the Holy Spirit. Christ has already accomplished everything for us. All we need to do is to accept it. As we'll explore later, the egalitarian Trinity does not negate roles and power differentials, be they human or divine. Often it is necessary to lead or to submit for the purposes of love, just as Jesus submitted to the Father and Spirit in order to redeem us.

Our relationships with each other were never meant to be identical, but they were always meant to be similarly characterized by God's love. In the Trinity each person is *uniquely related* to the others. Yet all of the relationships are *characterized identically* by God's sacrificial love, in which there is no permanent hierarchy of worth or authority. Any static hierarchy rejects mutual submission by placing one person permanently below another. Such a hierarchy is subordinationist and does not reflect the Trinity. As Christians we will always need leaders who exercise real power, yet it is not Christian to choose or to characterize such leaders on the basis of our world's fallen social ordering. Rather, we are to be like Jesus and choose leaders, male and female, who live like Jesus and are gifted by the Holy Spirit.

| LIVE LIKE IT MATTERS |

Working out what mutual submission looks like is difficult for us mortals. For starters, every situation is different. Also, the world is fallen and we have egos and blind spots. And we all have biases toward people who are different from us. We tend to lack faith that our sacrifices will be meaningful. In the face of this, Jesus taught us that service and leadership are the same. We must serve others, especially if we mean to lead others.

The world will not back Jesus up on this, so it is likely that your work, and maybe even your family or church, will not reward servant leadership. However, God will, every time. It is how we learn to love like Jesus loves. Mutual submission always looks like love. Yet we must come to grips with the reality that this side of heaven, love is sometimes one sided. It is often not reciprocated and can be taken advantage of, making it non-mutual. Accept this and do it anyway. Why? Because Jesus did it, and told us to do it. In doing so, we reveal ourselves to be his disciples, immersed in the Father, Son, and Holy Spirit. Through our servant leadership, God invites others into his love.

29 SCRIPTURE AND THE ACTUAL TRINITY

The picture that Scripture draws for us:
The mutual submission of the Trinitarian communion.

This model of the actual Trinity illustrates the submission of the Son and the Holy Spirit that we see in Scripture by simply incorporating the acts of creation, redemption, and sanctification into the mutual, eternal submission of the three divine persons. It is clearly seen once we view these divine actions throughout the biblical text as Trinitarian actions. Below I will outline the scriptural context, first broadly, and then in more detail. When looking at the model, the descriptors of "sending" and "giving" could be replaced with "submits" and "empowers" if you like, or other labels. In the divine perichoresis, the Trinity literally inspires itself, for who else would God look to for inspiration?

The Father is the Creator, yet the biblical account of creation does not begin with the Father. According to Genesis 1, it begins with the Holy Spirit hovering over the waters and initiating creation.[129] We can think of the Holy Spirit's movement as sending the Father, who creates through the divine power of the Son (the *Logos*).[130] The Son is the Redeemer, but according to the New Testament, redemption does not begin with the Son. It begins with the Father initiating redemption by sending the Son, who redeems through the divine power of the Holy Spirit. The incarnation, ministry, and resurrection of Jesus Christ are all through the power of the Spirit. The Spirit is the Sanctifier, but sanctification does not begin with him. It begins with the redemptive works of the Son, who sends the Spirit[131] and initiates sanctification through the power of the Father.[132]

The Bible has revealed this dynamic process to us. It is our temporal glimpse of the eternal God who exists as a self-giving

---

[129] Genesis 1:2
[130] John 1:3, Colossians 1:17
[131] John 15:26, 16:7, 20:21–23
[132] John 14–16, Acts 1:7, 2:33

communion of agape love. While I do not wish to validate this egalitarian model by proof-texting, it is helpful to reference some pertinent passages. The Scriptures and the Christian tradition recognize the Father as Creator, the Son as Redeemer, and the Holy Spirit as Sanctifier. Each divine act is understood as Trinitarian, in which all three divine persons are intimately involved, yet each act also has a primary actor immediate to the world—Father in creating, Son in redeeming, Spirit in sanctifying.

The Father is the immediate actor in creation. "Is he not your Father, who created you, who made you and established you?"[133] *Yet the Bible imagines the Holy Spirit as the initiator of creation.* "In the beginning, God created the heavens and the earth. Now the earth was formless and empty, darkness was over the surface of the deep, and the Spirit of God was hovering over the waters."[134] The Holy Spirit hovering over the waters precedes and initiates the Father's creative act. *Creation is by the Father, but it is through the power of the Son.* "All things came into being through him [the Son], and without him not one thing came into being."[135] The egalitarian model follows the biblical witness in imagining creation as initiated by the Holy Spirit, who empties into the Father and the Son. The kenosis of the Holy Spirit results in the sending of the Father for creation and the giving of divine power over creation to the Son.

The Son is the immediate actor in redemption. "Christ redeemed us from the curse of the law by becoming a curse for us."[136] *Yet the Bible portrays the Father as the initiator of redemption.* "And we have seen and do testify that the Father has sent his Son as the Savior of the world."[137] In the Gospels, Jesus often states that the Father has sent him.[138] The Gospels communicate that *redemption is by the Son, yet it is through the power of the Holy Spirit.* It is the Spirit who empowers the incarnation

---

[133] Deuteronomy 32:6

[134] Genesis 1:1–2 (NIV)

[135] John 1:3

[136] Galatians 3:13

[137] 1 John 4:13

[138] John 8:18 is one example

of Jesus,[139] his ministry,[140] and his resurrection.[141] This picture follows the biblical witness in portraying redemption as initiated by the Father, who empties into the Son and the Holy Spirit. The kenosis of the Father results in the sending of the Son for redemption and the giving of divine power over redemption to the Holy Spirit.

The Holy Spirit is the immediate actor in sanctification.[142] *Yet the Bible portrays the Son as the initiator of sanctification.* The redemptive act of the Son moves him to initiate sanctification through the sending of the Holy Spirit.[143] Jesus clearly predicts and performs this sending— stated explicitly in the Gospels of Luke and John, and also in Acts. *Sanctification is by the Holy Spirit, yet it is through the power of the Father.* Jesus acknowledges the Father's governing role in sanctification, often mentions that this sending is the promise of the Father, and clearly links the power of sanctification to the Father.[144] Jesus also speaks of the Spirit being sent by the Father through the Son; Jesus asks the Father, who in turn governs the sending of the Spirit through the Son.[145]

Jesus explains this in John: "When the Advocate comes, *whom I will send* to you from the Father—the Spirit of truth *who goes out from the Father*—he will testify about me."[146] Finally, Jesus tells us that the timing of the eschaton, which is the culmination of sanctification, is to be decided by the Father.[147] Our egalitarian model follows the biblical witness in imagining sanctification as initiated by the Son, who empties into the Holy Spirit and the Father. The kenosis of the Son results in the sending of the Holy Spirit for sanctification and the giving of divine power (of which all authority in heaven and earth had been given to him upon the resurrection) over sanctification to the Father.

---

[139] Matthew 1:18, Luke 1:35

[140] Luke 4:1, 14 is an example

[141] Romans 8:11

[142] 2 Thessalonians 2:13, and 1 Peter 1:2 are two examples

[143] Luke 24:49, John 15:26, 16:7, 20:22, Acts 2:33

[144] Besides the previously referenced, see John 17:17 and Acts 1:7–8

[145] John 14:15, Acts 2:33

[146] John 15:26, NIV (emphasis mine)

[147] Matthew 24:36, Mark 13:32

Let's return to the important fact that the Trinity as revealed to us in human history is not the complete picture of the eternal God. We see only what is revealed. The Trinity that is recorded in the Bible is but a finite glimpse. Yet it is an absolutely true glimpse of the eternal God, seen most completely in the person of Jesus, who is the image of the invisible God and the exact representation of God's being. No one has a full view, but the view we get in Scripture is one of giving and receiving love through mutual empowerment and submission. We see a God who freely pours out life while receiving new life, and who extends that life to us.

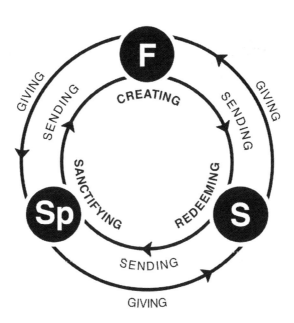

| LIVE LIKE IT MATTERS |

So what is the point of Christianity? What Jesus Christ reveals is that God is indeed with us. Yet this is not good news unless God is also on our side. God not only loves us, he also likes us. He is not only *willing* to save you, he *wants* to. *He became human permanently and did everything to accomplish victory over our sin and death.* No, he doesn't like everything you do, but deep down in your truest self, God made you good and is working within you to free you from captivity. God understands you at a human level, yet he has the power to transform your life at a divine level.

Eternally, God submits to and empowers Godself as Trinity. In Jesus, God submitted to human limitations. Through the resurrection and ascension, he has empowered humanity to enjoy God's eternal life. God is beyond you as Father, with you as Jesus, and in you as the Holy Spirit. God has chosen you! Say yes to God's yes to you. Just look at what God has done for you through Jesus. Say yes to the work of the Spirit within you. Pray this yes everyday. Live it. See it for others, and remind them of the dance of God extended to you.

30   TAKING TRADITIONAL BABIES OUT OF THE BATHWATER

We can keep the traditional descriptions when we see them within the larger, subordination free picture.

The model of the integrated and egalitarian Trinity imagines something larger and more dynamic than the static models of the past. *With a more expansive view we can keep many traditional elements of Trinitarian understanding while removing the factors that make them so problematic.* In other words, we can throw out the bathwater and keep the baby. The submission of the Son to the Father in the Bible remains true, but as part of the larger whole, that of the mutual submission of the Trinitarian communion. Likewise, the Father as the source of the Son and Spirit remains true, but only as part of the bigger picture in which the Trinitarian communion is its own eternal source. Taken out of the context of the larger whole, however, these elements create the conditions for Arianism, subordinationism, dual trinities, and the general irrelevance of the Trinity in Christian education. The result is the irrelevance of Christianity as a unique and meaningful worldview.

We have integrated the eternal and temporal trinities with a Christo-centric model of time and eternity. Now, with our egalitarian model of the Trinity, we have also eliminated the heresy of subordinationism in the Trinity without falling into modalism or tritheism. Each member of the Trinity freely depends on and submits to each other in the economy of our salvation. Jesus and the Spirit are not inferior because they submit to the Father and each other for the purposes of our redemption. Jesus submitted to his disciples by washing their feet—that did not make him inferior to them. God is love, and mutual submission characterizes this love.

Subordinationists are accustomed to distinguishing persons (human or divine) by fixed rank or status, and it might seem to them that eliminating fixed rank would eliminate the distinction among persons and make everyone the same. This is a misconception of egalitarianism, for equality of persons does not imply sameness. The

Trinity models diversity of persons with unique relations—in this way the Trinity is egalitarian and complementary. In a dynamic system, equality does not mean equal power or equal action in all circumstances, nor does it demand role uniformity. Yet power should always be used in service of the other if it is to be used in a godly way—that is, if it is to be an expression of God's love.

The symmetry of the model is likely to make subordinationists uncomfortable, for subordination is defined by asymmetrical power or status among persons. A critique of egalitarian symmetry I foresee is that it causes the relational dynamics within the Trinity to look identical. For example, a classical understanding of the relations would entail the Father breathing the Spirit and begetting the Son, with the Son being begotten and the Spirit being breathed. The Father has an active relation, while the Son and Spirit each have a passive relation. If in the model of the actual Trinity they are each actively giving and sending, submitting and empowering in perfect love, how then is each a distinct person?

In response I would say that the relational dynamics are similar because they are animated by the same agape love that constitutes the divine communion and that makes the Trinity one perfect being. If one person of the Trinity is its lone source, then you don't have a Trinity, but a monist God with two demigods. Second, in the egalitarian model unique roles and relations still characterize the actual Trinity of three distinct persons. This is clearly seen in the economy of our salvation with the Father as Creator, the Son as Redeemer, and the Holy Spirit as Sanctifier, yet since God is one in action, each action reveals the entire Trinity. Additionally, the Son remains the Son of the Father, the Father remains the Father of the Son, and the Spirit remains the Spirit of the Father and Son. These relations are what make each person unique.

It is worth noting at this point that the definition of *person* has changed over the centuries. Back in the fourth century when the doctrinal statements of three persons in one being were put forward—God's mind and will, what we now think of as *personality*—were thought of as corresponding more with the one being of God than with the three persons. The egalitarian relations of love are simply characteristic of the loving unity that is God. Seeing the three persons as having unique roles and relations which are each characteristically identical holds the paradox of personality between the one and the three.

We cannot peer into eternity and say precisely what makes the three persons distinct from each other apart from what has been revealed to us in time-space. For our understanding, then, the distinction among the Father, Son, and Holy Spirit is not found so much in how they uniquely relate to each other in eternity, for this we cannot know. *The distinction is found in how they uniquely relate to the world in and through each other, which characterizes but does not capture the eternal communion.* Father, Son, and Spirit each interact with the world distinctly through creation, redemption, and sanctification, yet it is all unified and characterized by one relational love.

Yet we must be careful not to take any one particular submission we see in time, mistake the snapshot for the whole movie, and then claim that the Trinity is asymmetrical this way within eternity. Subordination is justified in this way, and the practice ought to end. While the submission of Jesus to the Father is essential, it is not the entire picture we are given. The Father and the Spirit also submit and do not hesitate to give all to each other. The bottom line is this: God is a divine community expressed as love before the world was even created. And we are invited into this community through Jesus Christ. This is an amazing story—one we should be talking about!

| LIVE LIKE IT MATTERS |

Let's look at The Great Commission. Jesus said that "*all authority in heaven* and earth has been given to me." The Father gave the Son everything, total control of all eternity—*all* authority, on earth *and* heaven. Yet later we see that Jesus will give it all back (1 Cor. 15). Why? So that God can be all in all. Not so that the Father can be all in all, but so that the Trinity can be all in all. Father, Son, and Spirit freely giving and receiving from each other, including their relationship with us. No strings attached.

Is your love freely given? What do you expect in return? If you do expect something in return, even if it's just a thank-you note, then your gift was no gift at all, but rather an economic exchange. God's agape love is never about an exchange—it gives freely and demands nothing in return. But if we choose not to reciprocate then we cut ourselves off from divine life. Everything you have you were given. I know that culture says that you earned it all, but it is all grace. We must be willing to give it all away, even our very selves. We are not to hold out or hold back. Start by letting go of something small.

31 EAST AND WEST—HAVING IT BOTH WAYS

Reconciling the Eastern and Western Models.

One benefit of our integrated and egalitarian model is that it reconciles the Eastern and Western ideas of the Trinity, including the *filioque* clause. The Eastern Church (Orthodox Churches) generally understands the eternal Trinity in terms of perichoresis, and the temporal Trinity in terms of the Son and Holy Spirit being sent by the Father to the world. The Western Church (Catholic and Protestant Churches), unlike the Eastern, has traditionally understood the eternal Trinity in terms of the Holy Spirit being the bond of love between the Father and the Son. The Western view of the temporal Trinity is also different from the Eastern, in that it has a contentious addition, as found in later Western versions of the Nicene Creed, stating that the Holy Spirit is sent from the Father *and the Son. Filioque* simply means *and the Son* in Latin.

Sketched out, it all looks something like this.

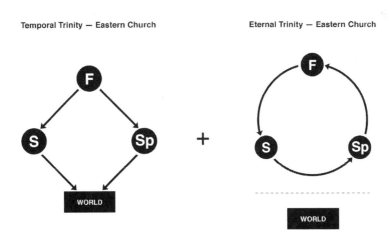

Figure 3: Eastern trinities

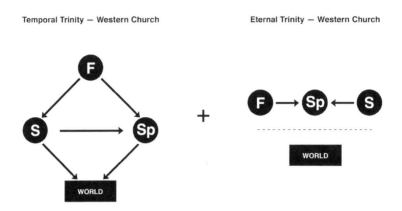

Figure 4: Western trinities

I strongly believe that both perspectives, and all four Trinitarian models, are true. They do not contradict each other, as one might think—it is just that each is rather incomplete. As the model of the Trinity portrays *(see Figure 8)*, the Holy Spirit is sent by the Son through the power of the Father. The Spirit comes to us from the Father and from the Son, yet it is one sending and not two. The East is right in that the Spirit comes to us by the Father. The West is right in that the Spirit also comes to us from (or through) the Son. Similarly, Scripture at times describes the Son as coming to us from the Father, while other times it describes the Son as coming to us from the Father and the Spirit. Both are true, as the Son comes to us by the Father through the power of the Holy Spirit. Of course the integrative and egalitarian leap is that the Father in creation is also sent by the Holy Spirit, through the power of the Son as Logos, through whom all things were created.

Here is a simplified sketch of the integrated and egalitarian Trinity that combines the dynamics of the East and West:

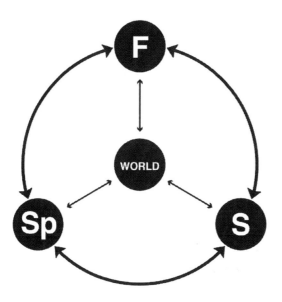

Figure 9: Combing East/West, Eternal/Temporal trinities

The diagram illustrates the truth of all four models, East and West, temporal and eternal, in one simple Trinity. God relates to Godself in eternity, and through creation, redemption, and sanctification, God also relates to us. It is the finite extension of the eternal dance of the Trinity. Everybody is right, but everybody is only partly right. The Western models clearly have problems. *Filioque* introduces asymmetry into the temporal Trinity unnecessarily while in the eternal Trinity the Holy Spirit is reduced to an impersonal force as the bond between the Father and the Son. The Eastern models are better in my opinion but still incomplete, as they are dis-integrated from each other and are less dynamic than the Western models.

All of the models are useful and true. I propose we combine them to portray a multi-directional perichoresis. In the self-giving love that is the Trinity, each divine person is sent and empowered by the others. This eternal perichoresis celebrates the one God who exists as a dynamic communion of love. If the Western *filioque* were amended and expanded along the lines of the Eastern perichoresis, then perhaps both East and West could acknowledge that while the Spirit is the bond of love between Father and Son, so too is the Father the bond of love between Son and Spirit, and the Son the bond of love between Spirit and Father. This love is extended to us in creation, made flesh for us in Christ, and will be fully realized for us in the eschaton. Come, Lord Jesus!

| LIVE LIKE IT MATTERS |

Martin Buber proposed that there are two kinds of human relationship, I-it and I-Thou. In I-it relationships, we objectify each other as things to be used. In contrast, I-Thou relationships are characterized by interpersonal openness to the other, in which our defensiveness and posturing cease. We do not demand anything from the other. Here we can transcend ourselves and become more of our true selves. Buber was Jewish, but he happened to capture the picture of the Trinity quite well, believing I-Thou was a reflection of God.

If we want to see God, we can indeed look to each other. We are not God, not at all, but God is in us, and between us, in the midst of our relationships. God exists through relationship, and so do we. When we truly encounter each other in agape love, we also encounter the life of God. Find a safe person and let down your masks and defenses. It's scary. Practice with God in prayer. Be real, but be open to the other. You will never transcend yourself if you don't.

32 ROLES AND RANKS
Why are you in charge?

If the one being of God exists as an act of mutual submission and empowerment among the Father, Son, and Holy Spirit, what does this say about role, rank, and hierarchy in human communities? After all, if the Trinity is the ultimate community, then equality among people should translate into the life of the Church. Even so, the realities of human organizations require what we think of as roles and/or ranks. Even in specific contexts where egalitarianism is a valued goal, everyone does not have equal say in all decisions, and everyone does not equally participate in all functions. So how does the egalitarian Trinity help us to define and live with role and rank in our relationships, churches, and other organizations?

Appeals to the Trinity to justify subordination are misguided, for in God there is no subordination of any kind. However, the Trinity does not imply that all distinctions of power and service are inherently wrong. God exemplifies persons who take on specific roles and functions in our creation, redemption, and restoration. Yet in their action there is a unity in which all three are always involved. Importantly, the submission that God demonstrates is voluntary and reciprocal. The Trinity portrays perfect egalitarianism within a dynamic relationality. Never does one demand submission from another. To submit in love and to be subordinated through force are as different as night and day.

The egalitarian model is helpful in that it incorporates God's mutual submission revealed in the Bible. The Father, Son, and Holy Spirit take on specific roles for the purposes of creation, redemption, and sanctification. *Real power differentials exist among them, not because any one of them is in any way less, but because they continuously pour out their power in submission to each other.* As we see with the earthly ministry of Jesus, the divine persons relate within temporary hierarchies where distinction in rank is present. However, these distinctions in power and/or role do not imply lesser status or any permanent asymmetry. Jesus took on the form of a servant, but this did not negate his status as fully God.[148] He also washed his disciples' feet, but that did not make him any less.

In response to a dispute among the disciples concerning who is the greatest, Jesus was explicit.

> The kings of the Gentiles lord it over them; and those in authority over them are called benefactors. But not so with you; rather the greatest among you must become like the youngest, and the leader like one who serves. For who is greater, the one who is at the table or the one who serves? Is it not the one at the table? But I am among you as one who serves.[149]

Christians are not to think of power, status, and authority in the subordinationist way in which the world regards them. Jesus served as God among us, because it is God's nature to do so. Human communities will always take on some form of social ordering. If this ordering places people on a ladder of worth where power is the primary concern, it is sinful, and it is subordinationism. If the ordering is a dynamic construct of mutual submission in which love is the primary concern, then it is a reflection of God. In God's agape, leading and serving are one and the same.

Jesus and the Spirit are equal to the Father, and yet they gladly submit to the him for our redemption and sanctification. They give up rank and power willingly out of love. This is a glimpse of the self-giving love of God, and this self-giving love *is* God. The glimpses we get in Scripture are snapshots of the divine perichoresis. The Father, Son, and Holy Spirit live in dynamic interdependence characterized by reciprocal submission and empowerment.

Godly community therefore involves mutual submission.[150] This is exactly what Scripture teaches us. We are called to submit to our leaders,[151] even as leaders are called to be like servants and submit to

---

148 Philippians 2:5–11
149 Luke 22:25–27
150 Ephesians 5:21
151 Hebrews 13:17, 1 Peter 2:13

those they lead.[152] Wives are called to submit to their husbands,[153] even as husbands are called to submit to their wives.[154] This does not imply that we are all the same. True community demands diversity of both leadership and social role.[155] We are all equal, yet we are not the same. Being equal and the same cannot be equated, but neither should difference ever be exploited to justify subordination.

A Trinitarian insight is key here: Role and rank are contextual and should exist in a dynamic system of mutual submission. Within such a system it may be contextually appropriate for a man to be over a woman, or for a woman to be over a man, or for a bishop to be over the laity, etc. Yet it would be a mistake to make a universal claim that a particular ordering is permanently how things are meant to be. To do so undermines our understanding of the Trinity at a fundamental level, for Jesus himself exists alongside the Father[156] even as he fully submitted to the Father during his ministry. And since it is the Trinity that is the mark of Christianity, subordinationist systems stand against the foundation of the Christian faith, as they stand against the nature of God.

As we legitimately resist abusive hierarchies, some advocate for an egalitarian leadership structure in which real power differences are to be avoided. This goal is noble and we should seek it, though attaining it may be impossible this side of heaven. Given the difficulty of achieving perfect egalitarianism, we must be careful not to gloss over the real power differences that always exist in a fallen world not perfectly characterized by God's love. We can idolize a completely organic and egalitarian congregation, which at its best is a holy longing for divine community. At its worst, it can be a reveling in chaos that causes more problems than it solves.

The egalitarian Trinity removes legitimization for hierarchy, but it certainly does not remove the need for contextually appropriate submission. Leadership should be used to advance the welfare of all, requiring a degree of

---

[152] Luke 22: 24–27
[153] Ephesians 5:22
[154] Ephesians 5:25
[155] Romans 12:3–8
[156] Philippians 2:6

organization in role and function. It is a mistake to use egalitarianism to justify chaos or harm, often the result of a leader neglecting his or her given responsibility. As the egalitarian Trinity shows us, all relationships have structure, but relational structure is dynamic, reciprocal, mutual, and appropriate to its context.

I have seen leaders and ministers misuse the principles of relationality and egalitarianism to deny the power, privilege, and position that their context gives them. This is another way of equating the notion of being equal with that of being the same. Abdicating responsibility to others while enjoying privileges others do not share is not what the Trinity reveals to us. Service, leadership, and taking responsibility as appropriate to the context is what the Trinity embodies.

Mutual submission will always demand some form of social structure. This structure may be a corrupt one of "lording over" and be found to be abusive and antithetical to divine community. Or it may be found to be a community of mutual service that expresses God's love. While God's love is easily characterized, there is no one-size-fits-all formula as to what love looks like in any given situation. There is therefore no one-size-fits-all formula to individual roles and church leadership structures, other than the principle of mutual submission in the service of others.

| LIVE LIKE IT MATTERS |

So how do we discern when to submit and when to lead, especially since they are two sides of the same coin? We love boldly. Some of us are more comfortable leading than others. Those of us who like to be in charge need to practice service, and those of us who find it safe to submit need to practice asserting leadership. And we all need a life that flows between the two. God has called you to lead somewhere, and this leadership must be in service to others. And God has called you to follow somewhere, looking out for the welfare of your leaders.

We need roles. We need leaders. We need servants. We need to be empowered. We all need to be all these things at the same time, because that's how we love. Yet we don't need the world's system of lording over each other to tell us what our roles, leaders, and service should be. We each need to discern with God and with our community what servant leadership in our context looks like. When in doubt, we look to Jesus, who has shown us the way.

33   THE GREAT INVITATION

The human network of relationships throughout history is a reflection of God. Just as God exists as an act of communion, we literally come into the world only through relationships. We understand the world and ourselves through such relationships. Just as each person of the Trinity pours his life out into the others, life on this earth comes about through similar sacrifice, the perpetual emptying of self for the nurturing of new life. Relationships define us. They determine our very being—first, in the sense that the Trinitarian relationship creates, redeems, and will restore the world, and second in that the human community co-creates us biologically and socially. Relationship links us back to the beginning and forward to the end.

Even our relationship with God is shaped within the human community. We are not the sole masters of our own destiny, no matter how many advertisements say otherwise. Our existence as individuals is paradoxically tied to the space between individuals, for interpersonal relationships require individuals, and individuals require interpersonal relationships. *Relationship defines us in total, for as the Trinity reveals to us, relationality is the ground of existence itself, where all being and becoming comes from and goes to.* Relationship is where all meaning and purpose are found in spite of sin and the enemy's desire to defile and deform. In Jesus this enemy is defeated, and through him we are invited into eternal life—the sin-free, self-giving relationship that is God. To reject this relationship is to choose hell—separation from God and others.

Though distorted by sin, our human communion makes up the image of God. History moves forward, the earth continues its annual journey around the sun, and there is much that is wrong with the cosmos. Alienation, sickness, and death are our constant companions. Suffering and injustice surround us like the air we breathe. So we tend to grasp onto whatever we can to help us make life more bearable, or to give us a little more control. We fail to pour ourselves out in love because we fear that the world will not reciprocate and pour back into us. Deep down, we feel alone and afraid. Acting out of these emotions further compounds human suffering.

Yet despite our brokenness, creation continues to be held together in Christ. He has taken on our condition and has overcome all barriers of separation. He promised that while the world may not reciprocate our love, his Spirit will indeed fill us, even unto eternal life. But we must surrender to the dance, the self-giving and receiving flow of divine life. We need to pour out in order to be filled. This is something we allow God to do in us as we respond to God's invitation to life. In doing so we find that we are not alone. Our being is tied up in God. Yet if we grasp onto our own life and refuse to share it—if we push God, and God in others, away—then in the end we are relinquishing life itself.

As Christians, we hope for the eschaton, when God will bring heaven down to earth, merging eternity and time-space. And that is what the Church is called to hope for and witness to, but in doing so we can miss the point of it all. For the unity between heaven and earth seen at the conclusion of the book of Revelation, the same unity that Paul speaks of in Ephesians 1:10 as already inaugurated in Christ, happens only through the redemptive work of Jesus. It is not just a future hope, but a present reality. God has assumed our humanity, submitting to and overcoming its limitations. In doing so, the dance of the Trinity has overcome our brokenness, inviting us to participate in the divine life.

Jesus conquered death and eliminated the gap between God and humanity so that every life could no longer be a broken image that ends in death, but rather a true image of God in which life poured out always brings abundant life. In Christ we are reconciled, and our true image is restored. This is the great invitation of the Gospel. It requires far more than mental assent to any doctrine, for it is a call to live our lives as a reflection of the Trinity—Father, Son, and Holy Spirit, giving and receiving everything on behalf of each other. It is the overflow of this love that created us, that sent Jesus to die and rise again to redeem us, and that will fully restore all things in the end.

To accept the great invitation is not just about receiving a ticket to heaven. It is a call to accept that God is among us now, in the midst of our human relationships, and to join God in pouring out our lives on behalf of each other. You see, in Jesus, God is always with us. Jesus was here in the flesh and he is here now through the Holy Spirit. If we take the Gospel seriously, we continue to find him in the midst of how we treat each other, in our everyday interactions with "the least of these." God is found in the midst of our relationships, for the good that exists in any relationship is a reflection of the fact that God *is* love. As God and as a human, Jesus sits at the right hand of the Father, representing that humanity belongs eternally with God.

What does it look like to trust in the Trinity? We would live our lives on behalf of one another, knowing that doing so will certainly bring us to our death, but it will also raise us to new life in Christ. In him, nothing can ever separate us from the love of God, for God is closer to us than we can even imagine. God is beyond us, yes, but is also with us, and within us, and if we consent, filling and flowing through us. The day will come when what has been begun by the Father and inaugurated in Jesus Christ will be completed by the Holy Spirit. On that day all will be in communion, and God will be all in all. Fear, death, and injustice will be vanquished by joy, life, and peace. This is our hope. As it says in Romans 8:18, our present sufferings are not even worth comparing to the glory that will be revealed in us. This glory is the reflection of the life of the Trinity.

To live in light of the Trinity is to accept the great invitation to love as God loves. It is the only Trinitarian thing to do. May we know the shared love of the God who is one and three, unity in diversity, personhood through relationship, Father, Son, and Holy Spirit. And may that love overflow in our lives.

| LIVE LIKE IT MATTERS |

The Trinity shows us that eternal life is shared life. We are not isolated individuals on this side of heaven, and we certainly won't be on the other side. Shared life requires thoughtful concern, not just for our families and those like us, but for people not like us. It extends to people with the wrong values and the wrong politics. Shared life means that we want what is best for all, not just for ourselves, our loved ones, and our tribe.

Shared life is taking care of creation on behalf of God who gave it to us to steward, and on behalf of others who come after us. It means that when we vote, we vote another's best interest above our own. It goes against everything the world stands for. But it will be the only reality in the new heaven and new earth. It would be best for everyone if we started practicing now. Assuming that you live in a democracy and you can vote in the next election, try to vote in the best interests of all instead of just those of yourself and your family. Doing so may or may not change your vote, but at least you'll be thinking in the right way, and voting for the right reasons.

APPENDIX 1
FOUR HAZARDS OF INTEGRATION

Things to avoid in any integrative understanding of the Trinity.

I see four hazards of integrating the concepts of the eternal and temporal trinities. We need to have a unified understanding for the Trinity to be practical, yet there are good reasons why it has been separated.

Hazard 1 – Subordinationism

When one person of the Trinity is viewed as less divine than another, then you have subordinationism. An integrated view needs to avoid subordinationism, for not only does it deny the Trinity by denying the equality of the divine persons, but it denies the real saving presence of God for us in the Son and Spirit. This makes the doctrine impractical and nonsensical. We can talk all we want about how God is Trinity, but if God is not three persons who are equally God, then our Trinity talk is meaningless, and we may as well give up on it. Groups like the Jehovah's Witnesses have done exactly this.

The submission of the Son during his earthly ministry can be read to imply that the Son and/or Spirit is permanently subordinated to the Father. The subordination can be functional (the Son or Spirit's *role* is less divine) or ontological (The Son or Spirit's *being* is less divine). This view comes from a picture of a Father who remains above it all, sourcing the Trinity we experience and calling the shots. Not being equal to God, the Son and Spirit come from the Father, simply obey him, and run interference between eternity and creation for him.

The first hazard of integrating the "trinities" is when we assume subordination within either the temporal or eternal trinities, for the subordination in one is transposed to the other. God as Trinity is a communion of mutual submission. If our picture of the Trinity is one where this submission is permanently or eternally one-sided, then the submitting members lack the divine essence and authority of the lording members. And the lording members demonstrate that service and submission are in fact not godly at all, the opposite of what Jesus reveals to us. Subordinationism makes all divine persons less than God, and God less than Trinity.

Subordinationism defines God in terms that reject the Trinity outright. If two persons are dependent and subsequent by nature, while the third is independent as possibly the source of the other two, the result is a tiered divinity with one ultimate God and two lesser gods. A Trinity with two members who are not full-fledged members is not a Trinity. Subordinationism simply does not work as a way to integrate the "trinities" without practically eliminating the Trinity altogether.

Hazard 2 – Static Egalitarianism

The second hazard of integrating the temporal and eternal trinities is the opposite of the first. This view denies the submission and dependence of the Son and Spirit as revealed in the Bible, painting over it in favor of a simple egalitarianism. There exists in the biblical text a tension between egalitarian and subordinationist relations when it comes to the Trinity. To claim perfect equality among the Father, Son, and Holy Spirit without reconciling the scriptures that uphold submission and dependence within the Trinity is an erroneous interpretation of God's revelation. Integration needs to show that the submission and dependence in the Trinity that Scripture reveals is part of the dynamic relationship that Father, Son, and Holy Spirit perfectly share—both in time and beyond it.

Hazard 3 – Pantheism

A third potential hazard of integration is collapsing God and the world into each other to the point that God cannot be distinguished from creation itself. By bringing together the temporal Trinity (God within time-space) with the eternal Trinity (God beyond time-space), it is possible to collapse the eternal into the temporal so that the distinction cannot be discerned. God becomes dependent on creation instead of the other way around. Whenever the Trinity is reduced to three aspects of creation, or history, or even revelation, pantheism is lurking at the door and the Trinity is at risk of becoming simply a metaphor or lens to understanding human experience.

Recent theologians have rightly rejected two separate trinities, and three general responses have emerged to Karl Rahner's Rule: "The economic Trinity is the immanent Trinity, and vice versa,".[157] The first is to maintain a strict classical distinction and not integrate at all (see Hazard 4 below). The second is to conflate them completely and risk pantheism. The third way, which I am partial to, is to put up a caution flag on the "vice versa" portion of Rahner's Rule. This is because the temporal Trinity, God who we experience in time, is not exhaustive of the nature of the eternal Trinity. While the temporal Trinity is indeed the eternal Trinity, God's revelation to us in time *communicates and characterizes, but does not completely capture* the divine essence.

Pantheism is a simple solution to the problem of integration, but it denies the scriptural witness that while God indeed exists within creation in some way, God also exists beyond creation and certainly is not constituted by creation itself. While pantheism is an error, those who claim that the eternal and temporal trinities must remain separate to avoid pantheism are not completely justified. Any meaningful understanding of the Trinity is grounded in God's revelation, and this revelation takes place, is recorded, and is understood within time and space. If total separation is true and necessary, then we truly and necessarily know nothing of who God is. Jesus is just a madman after all.

Hazard 4 – Not Integrating to Preserve God's Freedom

The fourth hazard is a defense against pantheism. By integrating the temporal and eternal trinities, we come to understand God in terms of God's action in time-space. Much ink has been spilt by theologians agonizing over this problem. We know God only through his revelation to us in time-space, yet for God to be God, he must be beyond his creation. If we fully integrate the eternal Trinity

---

[157] Karl Rahner, *The Trinity*, trans. Joseph Donceel (New York, NY: Herder and Herder, 1970), 24.

with the temporal Trinity, then we risk making God dependent upon creation. If all we can say about God is that he creates, redeems, and restores us in the economy of salvation, then such worldly processes become necessary for God to be God. Thus, God would not be *free* to create, but would be dependent upon creation and be Creator by *necessity.*

This problem cuts at two levels. First, it seems reasonable to conclude that God is the same God even had he not created the universe. God is free to create, he is not forced to, and neither is God eternally co-substantial with the world in some way (like most contemporary philosophy argues). The pickle we are in is that the Trinitarian relations of any integrated view must still work, make sense, and be the same both for reality as we know it (an integrated or temporal Trinity), as well as if God had never created anything (the eternal Trinity only). Those who insist on God's freedom and sovereignty in this way have a point worth keeping in mind.

The solution requires an embrace of the double paradox of Jesus. Then we can see that the Trinitarian relations are the same in eternity and in time, such that the triune being is simply expressed in the world as the sacrificial extension, or overflow, of the eternal love of God. As Jesus makes clear, God is willing to condescend to our level. God chooses this path freely in love, and God desires to extend the divine life to us.

The second level regarding God's freedom involves a more severe reliance on classical commitments. Here, an understanding of the eternal God who has any real links to creation, or that is based on our experience of God in time, implies God's dependency on creation. The worry is that this would effectively deny God's freedom—or sovereignty—by implying that God would not be the same had God never made creation.[158] Those who posit this theory tend to demand that a stark distinction be maintained between the eternal and temporal trinities, believing that God can only be defined, essentially, in absolute terms beyond created time-space.

---

[158] Paul D. Molnar, *Divine Freedom and the Immanent Trinity: In Dialogue With Karl Barth and Contemporary Theology* (New York, NY: T&T Clark, 2002).

In this line of thinking, any view of the eternal and temporal trinities as the same Trinity—that is any integrated view at all—would be an error. For by linking the Trinity to creation, the metaphysical priority of protecting God from dependence upon his creation is violated. This position runs parallel to the view that one of God's primary attributes is immutability—a totally unchanging nature. To prevent bringing about any change in God upon the incarnation of Jesus and to keep the eternal Trinity pure, one would need a separate temporal Trinity to protect the eternal Trinity. If you bring the trinities together, then the apparent mutability of the temporal Trinity infects the immutability of the eternal Trinity.

While the concern is sincere, God's freedom and sovereignty are not threatened by all integrated models, nor are they threatened should God choose to have real relationship with creation. Relationships of love constitute the Trinitarian communion, and the person of Jesus reveals this eternal love to us within time. While God is certainly unchanging in his character and essence, I doubt that immutability is God's primary attribute. We cannot escape the core Christian belief that in Jesus, God has freely chosen in an act of sacrificial love to identify with humanity and with all creation. This act reveals that the nature of Jesus is both fully God and fully human. From God's eternal perspective, then, neither the character nor the nature of God necessarily changes upon creation, nor even upon the incarnation of Jesus. *As the Bible makes clear, this act of love was freely chosen by the Trinity from eternity.*[159] *The incarnation is revealed to us in time, but it is an eternal (beyond time) reality of God the Son.* Hence, the double paradox of Jesus informs our solution.

It is one thing to define God's being in terms of *dependency* to the world. It is quite another to define God in terms of *relationship* to the world, a relationship in which God, from eternity, freely chooses to identify with us in time. God in freedom has chosen to create, redeem, and sanctify the world. Thus, it is not God who is dependent on us, but we who are dependent on God to create, sustain, and extend divine relationship to us. The scriptural witness is the story of

---

[159] 2 Timothy 1:9, Titus 1:2

how God chooses exactly such a relationship, at great cost to Godself. God has chosen to pour Godself out for the world in love. This is who God is in eternity, pouring himself out in the dance of the Trinitarian communion.

In God's self-giving love, God has *chosen* to be *affected* (moved to feel or act) by us. Indeed, this choice would seem to be a requirement of agape love that is God. We see this with Jesus on the cross—God is clearly affected by the world. Yet God's being and character are in no way *effected* (changed) by the world. God has the choice, and in God's unchanging character, God always chooses love. The problem to be solved is not how to protect God's freedom from creation. Rather, the obstacle is to properly define God's relationship to time and eternity using the actual Trinity vs. several trinities.[160]

I believe that all four hazards of an integrated Trinitarian model are overcome by adequately defining God's relationship to time and eternity—through Jesus. Each model comes from either totally collapsing time into eternity, or from keeping time and eternity totally isolated. But what if time and eternity are themselves distinct, while the Trinity exists both within and beyond time-space, making either an absolute separation or a complete conflation of time-space and eternity both false understandings? And what if the person of Jesus, by being fully in both, brings them together for us?

What is revealed to us of God and what we experience of God, while being genuinely God, is never the entirety. By way of analogy—my experience of my next-door neighbor is real, though it is never an exhaustive experience of who he is. If this is true, then it applies infinitely more so to our experience of God. This experience of God is real, though never exhaustive of God. While our experience of the revelation is finite, the Trinity as revealed in time and space is still the same transcendent, eternal God of the universe.

There are not two trinities; it is just that there is a gap between how we come to know God (the temporal Trinity), and who God is

---

[160] Robert W. Jenson, *The Triune Identity* (Eugene, OR: Wipf and Stock, 2002), 125–26.

beyond our experience (the eternal Trinity). The distinction is not unlike how we come to know anyone. A person *is*, and a person *reveals* his or herself to us. The revelation characterizes, but does not capture the essence of that person. There is much more to the person. Even so, it would be nonsense to say after seeing the person "That was not so and so, just a finite revelation of himself." No, it was the actual person. Our knowledge of God comes from the temporal Trinity, yet the source of that knowledge comes from the eternal Trinity. *I conclude that with God the distinction is a necessary result of our finite perspective. It is not a distinction within the Trinity itself, or a distinction between "trinities."*

APPENDIX 2

INTEGRATIVE AND EGALITARIAN MODELS?

The triumphs and failings of the LaCugna and Jenson proposals, and requirements of a complete model.

A good model of the Trinity needs to be integrative. That is, it needs to portray how God beyond creation is the same God who is in relationship with creation, and it needs to do this without making God dependent upon creation to be God. A good model also needs to be egalitarian. It should illustrate the equality of the three divine persons, who are each fully God. Finally a good model needs to be dynamic, showing the submission and dependence within the Trinity that we see in the Scriptures without succumbing to a static subordinationism. Quite a task! Usually one priority takes away from the others.

I believe that the model set forward in this book does just this. Yet I stand on the shoulders of those who have come before me. I have been informed by the models of Robert Jenson and Catherine Mowry LaCugna. Although in the end I do not believe that they achieve all of the above goals.

In *God for Us: The Trinity and Christian Life,* Catherine Mowry LaCugna presents an integrated model. LaCugna illustrates the dynamic action of the Trinity chiastically. As she explains:[161]

> [the chiastic model] expresses the one ecstatic movement of God outward by which all things originate from God through Christ in the power of the Holy Spirit, and all things are brought into union with God and returned to God. There is neither an economic nor an immanent Trinity.[162]

---

[161] LaCugna, *God for Us: The Trinity and Christian Life,* 223.
[162] Ibid.

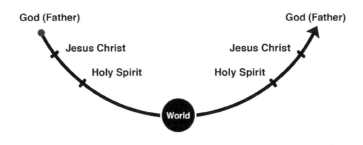

Figure 10: LaCugna Model

LaCugna seems to avoid the issue of whether and how God exists both within and beyond time and simply affirms that the eternal Trinity is indeed the temporal Trinity that we experience in the economy of our salvation. In this way the model integrates the eternal and temporal trinities. Her detractors accuse her of latent pantheism, one of the 4 hazards of integration, making God in history the totality of the eternal God. It is unclear to me if she goes this far in her integration. In my opinion, however, she definitely does not put forward an egalitarian model of the Trinity.

LaCugna argues that God, who is love, does not promote inequality or subordination within the Trinity. Yet in her model, the Father is the ontological source from whom the Son and the Spirit originate. Building on the work of Karl Rahner, she draws the Son coming into being from the Father, with the Spirit then coming from the Father and Son, who then bring the world into being. The second half of the chiasm incorporates God's historical redemptive acts, in which all things return through the Holy Spirit to Jesus Christ, and finally to the divine source of the Father, where all things will exist in the life of the Trinity. In this picture, the Son and Spirit are clearly subordinated to the Father. She even gives the Father the label of "God" to the exclusion of the Son or Spirit.

While LaCugna's model is integrative and it creatively brings together aspects of Catholic and Orthodox thinking, she equates God with the Father in a way that implies that the Son and the Holy Spirit are not fully God. While LaCugna would not want to suggest inequality among the three divine persons, her model upholds the functional subordination inherent in many classical theologies of the Father. She is different from classical thinkers in that she prioritizes the temporal Trinity, yet by integrating it with the eternal Trinity, she transposes the functional subordination of her limited view of the temporal Trinity back into the eternal Trinity, yielding an ontological subordination. She says,

> In the Bible, in early creeds, in most liturgical doxologies and Eucharistic prayers, as well as in Greek theology, "God" and "Father" are synonyms. God the Father is *ho theos,* the Uncreated Creator, Unoriginate Origin of everything that is. God the Father is the font of divinity, source of Word and Spirit. The biblical and creedal notion of redemption is that it originates with God the Father and is realized in Christ, through the power of the Holy Spirit.[163]

While we certainly ought to equate the Father with God as the Uncreated Creator, we often do so in a way that suggests that the Son and the Spirit are not also equated with God. LaCugna is on solid ground in using traditional language within the Orthodox and Catholic Churches. Theologians from Nicaea onward have argued that derivation of being does not imply difference in being. True enough, yet derivation from another does imply subordination. The biblical witness does not demand subordination, even if it has some standing in tradition. The Trinity is derived from the Trinity, not from the Father alone.

Beyond dislike of the Trinity, there is no compelling reason why we should settle for subordination within the Godhead. "God" and "Father" are indeed synonyms in our tradition, yet "Jesus" and "Spirit" are also synonyms for God, even if our tradition has sometimes been ambivalent on this point on account of liking a little subordinationism in our theology. If God is synonymous with the

---

[163] Ibid., 215.

Father to the exclusion of the Son and Spirit, then we lose the Trinity. God becomes a Father who is eternally unrelated to us, and we end up alone with no God to save us or indwell us.

LaCugna is correct that "the biblical and creedal notion of redemption is that it originates with God the Father and is realized in Christ, through the power of the Holy Spirit."[164] This does not require that the divinity of the Son and Spirit themselves originate with the Father, as opposed to the Trinitarian communion itself. I do not believe that LaCugna would have explicitly argued for subordinationism—she was an egalitarian—but her model implicitly argues it with vigor. Correctly representing the Trinity requires models in which the Father, Son, and Spirit, while not the same, are all equally God. LaCugna's model can be commended for its simplicity and integration, yet we require a truly egalitarian model.

Robert Jenson, in *The Triune Identity: God According to the Gospel,* goes another way in a creative attempt to solve the problems of disintegration and subordination in our thinking on the Trinity. Jenson's model portrays the Son (S) in the center of an oval with a yin-yang appearance. It labels the Father (F) as "Unoriginate" and labels the Spirit (Sp) as "Unsurpassed." The active and passive relations among the three divine persons are added in line with God's revelation in Scripture.[165]

Taking cues from the Cappadocian Fathers, Jenson takes the traditionally vertical relations depicting the Father, Son, and Spirit descending from eternity into time, and turns them sideways, yielding a horizontal model. This alignment allows the Trinitarian relations to be portrayed along our historical timeline, with the Father at the Beginning and the Spirit at the End, who together comprise the parenthesis of eternity that envelopes time. The Son is in the middle, within time itself. Jenson includes both the active and passive relations, as they both equally characterize divine activity. The Father "begets" the Son is replaced with a less problematic "intends," while

---

[164] Ibid.
[165] Jenson, *The Triune Identity*, 143.

the Son "is intended" by the Father. The Father also "gives" the Spirit as the Spirit "is given" by the Father. These first two sets of relations originating with the Father satisfy the traditional relations in which the Father is "Unoriginated" at the "Beginning."

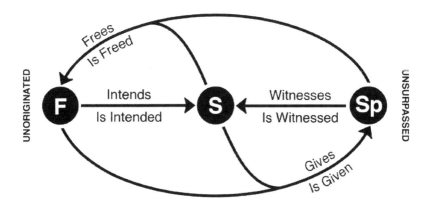

Figure 11: Jenson Model

Jenson believes that the classic depictions are subordinationist and result from a preoccupation with finding God, and more specifically the Father, at the Beginning. He says that "there can be no conception of the origin of the Son or the Spirit. Both are simply eternal as God is eternal."[166] Yet not wanting to completely lose the notion of the Father as Unoriginate, he draws two more sets of relations back to the Father and the Son from the Spirit, attempting to balance out the model and make it egalitarian. The Spirit "witnesses" to the Son, while the Son "is witnessed" by the Spirit, and the Spirit "frees" the Father (from a static, timeless eternity), while the Father "is freed" by the Spirit. The Spirit is placed at the End, the eschaton, and is labeled "Unsurpassed," counterbalancing "Unoriginate."

On its face, this model is integrative and egalitarian, but we have

---

[166] Ibid., 69.

to make some problematic assumptions. Jenson's work forces us to ask the question: Why not think of the end as both the source and goal of all things, rather than the beginning? Jenson is an eschatological theologian, so we need a quick reminder of what I call eschatological theism. In general, this view sees God as both within and beyond time-space, just as I have been proposing, as opposed to the classical view (God is absolutely beyond time-space) and the open view (God is absolutely within time-space).

Eschatological theism sees God as both within and beyond time—yet not through Christ's dual nature, but through the separation of God's being. It envisions the Father who is eternal, the Son who becomes wholly temporal, and the Spirit who is paradoxically both. The Spirit is the bond between Father and Son, and he will bring Father and Son back together at the eschaton when time and eternity are incorporated together. This unity was inaugurated at the resurrection of Jesus.

Like open theism, eschatological theism also has an open, undetermined future. The paradox (or problem) here is that this open future will redeem the past by determining what it has been, altering the past when necessary. According to Jenson and others, the eschaton becomes the ontological or metaphysical basis for originating and determining the Beginning itself, which is how the Unsurpassed Spirit eliminates the subordination of the Unoriginate Father. Jenson paints a beautiful picture of the eschaton where what is promised is neither a timeless eternity nor something that will be succeeded by other states, but simply divine love itself.[167]

Jenson's model is brilliant, but it suffers from many weaknesses. First, it is potentially tritheistic in that the temporal Son is split from the eternal Father, to become one God again only upon the eschaton. This is why in eschatological models the eschaton *must* determine the past and God's unity retroactively; if it did not, then the Father and Son would be separate beings, which is clearly tritheism. For this reason the model is not sufficiently integrative: the temporal Trinity is not at present the eternal Trinity—they are integrated only upon the

---

[167] Ibid., 171–173.

eschaton. That makes the eschaton all the more wonderful, but the present all the more terrible, for at present there is no actual Trinity, except in the future's retroaction.

In this way a second problem is that Jenson's model seems to be a reverse form of classical determinism. Rather than history being predetermined, it is post-determined. In synthesizing various eschatological theologians such as Moltmann, Pannenberg, Jenson, and himself, Ted Peters explains that it is only in the eschaton that the temporal Trinity becomes the eternal Trinity, and that the future will determine what we have been.[168] Yet I do not think that the eschaton as described in the Bible post-determines time-space—the past—in order to redeem it and incorporate it into eternity. And if it does, is not then the genuineness of the open future and free will simply a charade? For me it raises not only the question of how the Trinity matters in the present, but how anything at all matters in the present.

The third problem is that subordination remains in place. The emphasis on the Holy Spirit at the eschaton seems subordinationist in that the Spirit is the metaphysical principle that retroactively determines who God is as Trinity, including the Unoriginate Father. Yet even if the Father and Spirit are egalitarian, the subordination of the Son is not removed from the classical depiction at all. He is now ontologically subordinate not only to the Father, but also to the Spirit. Egalitarianism is not quite achieved here.

Fourth, Jenson relies heavily on viewing God as Spirit to make everything work out. He incorrectly states that "the only definition of God in Scripture is that God is Spirit."[169] This allows Jenson to give the Spirit divine priority, yet this Spirit is lacking any personhood. Jenson prefers the terms "identities" over "persons" when talking about the Trinity.[170] Jenson equates (or reduces) the Spirit to God's future and our future in God, where the future Spirit is metaphysically the bond between Father and Son, God and

---

[168] Ted Peters, *God as Trinity: Relationality and Temporality in the Divine Life* (Louisville, KY: Westminster John Knox Press, 1993), 178–179.

[169] Ibid., 167.

[170] Ibid., 105–111.

humanity. This strikes me as more philosophically binitarian than biblically Trinitarian.

Fifth and finally, the model suffers from an overemphasis on Augustine and Hegel's self-conscious analogies of the Trinity as one person with three inner relations (really two self-reflections, in my opinion) as opposed to a Trinity of three inter-relating persons who exist as one being through an eternal act of love. In line with Western philosophy, there is an over reliance on the absolute Subject of God, in which the Father is Subject, the Son his Object, and the Spirit the discovery of Godself as object.[171] While a brilliant Christianization of Hegelian and process philosophy (inasmuch as I understand it), Jenson's model is not in my opinion sufficiently grounded in Scripture and the person of Jesus, sufficiently egalitarian, or sufficiently integrative.

Giving primacy to the boundary event of the eschaton above the other boundary events of creation and Christ casts into doubt either God's relationship to time-space through Jesus, or God's relationship to Godself. It also leaves us again with two trinities by having an egalitarian Trinity upon the eschaton and a subordinationist Trinity in time, which will be united retroactively upon the eschaton. In the end, this is not an egalitarian model in which all three persons of the Trinity are equally God. Jenson certainly gets us thinking creatively, but I think that instead of viewing the Father as Unoriginate and the Spirit as Unsurpassed, we should instead see how the Trinity itself— Father, Son, and Holy Spirit—is its own Unoriginate Source and Unsurpassed Nature. We get there by letting go of our notion that God is one person with three manifestations, and embracing the paradox that God is three persons in one being.

---

[171] Ibid., 144–145.

APPENDIX 3

ETERNALLY BEGOTTEN?

There is no Scriptural support for the Son's begotten-ness.

The Arian controversy initiated the first ecumenical council in Nicaea in the year 325. From this council we received the Nicene Creed.[172] It is from this creed that we inherit an interesting piece of theology—the eternal begotten-ness of the Son. I grew up with this funny word *begotten*, for the King James Version of John 3:16 hung on the family room wall. Here it is in the creed:

> … We believe in one Lord, Jesus Christ,
>> the only Son of God,
>> eternally begotten of the Father,
>> God from God, Light from Light,
>> true God from true God,
>> begotten, not made,
>> of one being with the Father. …

Begotten is the equivalent of *born of,* especially in reference to a male parent. You may already be aware that in nearly all of our modern translations of the Bible, the phrase that once read "only begotten" as found in John 3:16 and other verses in older English translations has been replaced with "only" or "one and only." This is because it is now the complete scholarly consensus that the Greek word in question, "μονογενής" (*monogenes*), definitely means "only" or "only one of its kind" and definitely does not mean "only begotten."[173] "Only begotten" is not in the Greek, but the phrase has

---

[172] Revised in 381 at the first council of Constantinople. This is sometimes called the Niceno-Constantinopolitan Creed.

[173] "A Greek-English Lexicon of the New Testament and Other Early Christian Literature," ed. Frederick William Danker (Chicago: The University of Chicago Press, 2000), 658.

problematically made its way from the Nicene Creed into subsequent translations of the Bible, and ultimately into our understanding of the nature of the Son of God.

It was the intention of Nicaea to clearly counter Arian teaching and concisely state that the Son is co-eternal and of the exact divine being as the Father. To make the point, Nicaeans used language not in the Scriptures in saying that Jesus is "eternally begotten" of the Father.[174]—"eternally" to refute the Arian claim that Jesus was created at any point in time or sequence prior to our creation, and "begotten" to refute the Arian claim that Jesus has a being or nature in any way different from the Father, or anything less than full divinity. Thus, in the creed we get "eternally begotten of the Father, God from God, Light from Light, true God from true God, begotten, not made, of one being with the Father."

The first Latin translations, the Old Latin, correctly translated the Greek *monogenes* ("only, or only one of its kind") to the Latin *unicus* ("only"). If the original Greek had been meant to denote "only begotten," then the correct word would be *monogennetos* ("only begotten").[175] The reason we used the term *only begotten* stems from the early Greek apologists, who first used the term in reference to the Son. In doing so they planted the seeds of Arianism, giving language to Arianism's search for a middle-realm being.[176] Later, it was ironically the Nicene Fathers who gathered ideas of begotten-ness around the word *monogenes*.[177]

Soon after Nicaea, Jerome was commissioned to translate a new Latin version of the Bible, the Latin Vulgate. Jerome's translation changed *unicus* to *unigenicus* ("only begotten"), though only in the messianic passages. Jerome's probable intention was to refute Arianism, then a raging heresy, by inserting the language of Nicene

---

[174] Colin Gunton, "And in One Lord Jesus Christ ... Begotten Not Made," *Pro Ecclesia* 10, no. 3 (2001): 262.

[175] Ibid.: 213–14.

[176] Jenson, *The Triune Identity: God According to the Gospels*, 91.

[177] R.L. Roberts, "The Rendering of 'Only Begotten' in John 3:16," *Restoration Quarterly* 16, no. 1 (1973): 10.

orthodoxy.[178] Yet it seems clear that Jerome read the Nicene concept of eternally begotten into *monogenes*.[179] Jerome's Latin Vulgate with its incorrect notion on the Son's "begotten-ness" became the standard translation in the West for over a thousand years. Since we know that the original Greek texts—and the original Latin texts after them—never used the term "begotten" when referring to Jesus, the error has recently been corrected in modern translations.

Monogenes, the word we actually find in the Bible concerning the sonship of Jesus, correctly denotes a *unique manner of being,* as it literally means "the only one of its kind." Inserting "begotten" denotes something radically different, for it implies a *unique manner of coming into being.* The concept of Jesus' "coming into being" would seem to immediately support Arianism. The Nicene Christians didn't mean it that way, as they understood the Son's begotten-ness as eternal. Being eternal, the being of Jesus always *is.*

This serves as a lesson in reactionary theology. In confronting Arianism, the Nicene Christians ended up arguing on their opponents' terms: Instead of using the language of Jesus and the writers of the New Testament, in which the Son is fully God and in which the Father and Son are one, they played the Arian game in trying to describe how the Son is derived from the Father. It is certainly true that the Son's being comes from the communion of the Trinity—and his being eternally begotten of the Father can be a part of this larger whole of the Trinity constituting Godself. Alone however, "eternally begotten" implies that the Son is either ontologically or functionally inferior to the Father in that his being is derived exclusively from the Father, while the Father is underived.

Similarly, we should not use the sonship of Jesus as proof of subordination. Jesus is not a son to the Father in the same way that any other human is a son to his father. Human language about God is always by way of analogy. Our best attempts describe what God is like, but our language always falls short, for God is also always unlike

---

[178] Dale Moody, "God's Only Son: The Translation of John 3:16 in the RSV," *Journal of Biblical Literature* 72, no. 4 (1953): 214–16.

[179] Ibid.: 10–12.

our human analogies in some respects. On earth Jesus related to the Father, in human terms, *as a son to a father*, and therefore used those titles in describing their loving relationship. The Father is not, humanly speaking, literally Jesus' father as the Trinity also exists eternally, as one perfect being beyond creation. To take the metaphor literally, we'd also have to wonder when the Father, like other human fathers, would die of old age. While we rightly understand the Trinitarian relationship in terms of family, it doesn't make sense to take an analogy from creation and make it a literal representation of the eternal God. Doing so is, in fact, idolatry.

We should then be careful using "begotten" or the phrase "eternally begotten" in referring to the sonship of Jesus, as there is no biblical language supports it. Yet the Nicene tradition is so esteemed that removing the language entirely may not be wise in all contexts. I am aware that a similar argument can be made against the word "Trinity," as it also is not used in Scripture to describe God. The question we have to ask is this: What do the analogies of Scripture that describe God depict, and what does the full scope of Scripture imply? Scripture clearly portrays the Trinity. It does not depict the Son's eternal begotten-ness (his coming into being *as God*). The incarnation indeed depicts that the Son became human, but it certainly does not show that the Son *came into being*, either at his incarnation or at any other point in history or divine sequence.

It is worth noting that the context for the sending of the Son by the Father is the revelation of Jesus within time-space, not eternity. "For God so loved the world that he gave his *only unique* Son, so that everyone who believes in him may not perish but may have eternal life."[180] Our forbears have taken the sending of the Son in time, changed it to begotten-ness, and then moved that begotten-ness from time to eternity. The end result has been a more nuanced form of Arianism. Instead of an eternal Father and a temporal-ish Jesus as with Arianism, you end up with an eternal Trinity and a temporal-ish Trinity that function in the same way. The effect is that Arianism and this version of orthodoxy become a distinction without a difference.

---

[180] John 3:16

APPENDIX 4

WHAT ABOUT SUBJUGATION IN 1 CORINTHIANS 15:20-28?

It's really a picture of mutual submission

In this passage Paul is describing how we will be incorporated into the life of the Trinity through the resurrection. Our resurrection is in and through Christ's resurrection. At the Great Commission we learn that the Father placed all things under Jesus—Jesus said that all authority, even all the authority of heaven, had been given to him. At the eschaton, the Spirit will incorporate the world with heaven, and all things will be one in Christ. So how then will all things be one in God? Jesus and the Spirit will continue the perichoretic dance of the Trinity and give it all back to the Father. That is what Paul is showing us in 1 Corinthians 15:20-28.

Verse 28 needs some unpacking. ". . . then the Son himself will be made subject to him who put everything under him, so that God may be all in all."[181] The word traditionally translated as "subject" simply means that he submits, not that he is any less God. All the verses in the New Testament that tell us to submit to one another use the same word (in verb form) that we see here with the term "subject." The notion that Jesus is eternally subjugated to the Father takes this verse too far. First of all, the word does not mean subjugated as we think of it in English nowadays—it simply means submission. Second, even if subordinationist readings of this verse are correct, then it would imply that Jesus is currently *not* subject to the Father. This would happen later, so there is a back and forth going on anyway. Third, the scholarly consensus is that the verse should be understood to mean that Jesus is willingly submitting to the Father, not that he is being forced to submit, as some translations imply with a rendering like "made subject to him."

The point of the passage is Paul's conclusion: "so that God may

---

[181] 1 Corinthians 15:28 (NIV)

be all in all." It speaks to our inclusion into the life of the Trinity in which God is the God of everything, not just in principle, but in practice. God is already complete, but creation is separate from God, making creation incomplete. Through the act of Christ, creation and God have come together in Jesus. Upon the eschaton, the Spirit will bring God and creation together fully. And intimacy with the Father will become a reality for us, for the Son and Spirit will give their present authority and presence over creation back to the Father. We already know the Father in and through the Son and Spirit, for they are one being. Yet at the restoration of all things, the Father will no longer be distant from us and fallen creation. We will be beautifully reunited with our Creator God. And God (Father, Son, and Holy Spirit) will be all in all.

APPENDIX 5

HOW ABOUT ALL THOSE SUNDAY SCHOOL ANALOGIES?

They're all right. They could be righter.

If you grew up going to church, then you likely had the Trinity explained to you with analogies far simpler than the models in this book. So what about them? Is the Trinity like an egg, or a clover, or matter, or a family? The answer is that most of these analogies are appropriate in explaining *aspects* of what the Trinity is like. Yet we need to be aware of how they also misrepresent the Trinity, of how each analogy is very unlike God.

Figure 2: The Double Paradox With the Outer Rim (page 44), illustrates 10 basic misunderstandings of the Trinity that we can fall into when we fail to hold the double paradox of Jesus. While most of the following analogies are helpful to a point, they also rely on one or more of the 10 views on the rim of misunderstanding. Here is a list of some common analogies along with their shortcomings:

- Is the Trinity like an egg? Three parts making one whole, with a shell, white, and yolk?
  - o Yes, but no (this is partialism).

- Is the Trinity like a clover? Three leaf stems coming together to make one plant?
  - o This is better than the egg analogy (but still partialism or monism). One stem is not wholly a clover, nor is the whole three unique clover persons.

- Is the Trinity like matter, say water? Three states of one substance being able to exist as either a solid, liquid, or gas?
  - o Yes, but no (this is definitely modalism). Water can be in only one state at a time.

- Is the Trinity like space? One field with three dimensions of height, depth, and width?
  - o This is better than the matter analogy because all three exist simultaneously and they interpenetrate each other (but it is still partialism or monism).

- Is the Trinity like the sun? One object with three aspects—source, heat, and light?
  - o Yes, but no (this is subordinationism, Arianism, partialism and monism). The source (the sun itself) creates the heat and the light, and the heat and light are hard to distinguish.

- Is the Trinity like time? One experience with three components of past, present, and future?
  - o This is better than the sun analogy but it depends on your view of time. At any rate I think that all views of time would fall short in some respect.

- Is the Trinity like a man with three relations (he is a father, a husband, and a son)?
  - o This is modalism again. The Trinity is three persons, not one person with three roles or modes of being.

- Is the Trinity like a family? 3 people who exist together as a father, mother, and child?
  - o This is tritheism. The family is not one being and will, as the Trinity is.

- Is the Trinity like a spoken word? One word with three communicative acts: thought, sounded, and heard?
  - o This is a good relational example, but it is either Arianism, modalism, partialism or tritheism. Either the thought creates the spoken and heard aspects, or else they are three modes of a single speech act. Or they are three separate parts that form one act, or they are three separate things that may or may not be

united under some higher, fourth thing.

The bottom line is that analogies are helpful and necessary, but beware the single analogy! No one picture or analogy can grasp the full mystery and paradox of the Trinity. It is like trying to stuff the source of all reality itself into a box.

BIBLIOGRAPHY

"A Greek-English Lexicon of the New Testament and Other Early Christian Literature." Edited by Frederick William Danker. Chicago: The University of Chicago Press, 2000.

Bilezikian, Gilbert. "Hermeneutical Bungee Jumping: Subordination in the Godhead." *Journal of the Evangelical Theological Society* 40, no. 1 (1997): 57–68.

Boyd, Gregory A. *Satan and the Problem of Evil: Constructing a Trinitarian Warfare Theodicy.* Downers Grove, IL: InterVarsity Press, 2001.

Boyd, Gregory A. *God of the Possible: A Biblical Introduction to the Open View of God.* Grand Rapids, MI: Baker Books, 2000.

Breen, Mike, and Steve Cockram. *Building a Discipling Culture.* Pawleys Island, SC: 3 Dimension Ministries, 2009.

Budde, Michael L. "Collecting Praise: Global Cultural Identities." In *The Blackwell Companion to Christian Ethics*, edited by Stanley Hauerwas and Samuel Wells, 123–37. Malden, MA: Blackwell Pub., 2004.

Chan, Simon. *Liturgical Theology: The Church as Worshiping Community.* Downers Grove, IL: IVP Academic, 2006.

Documents of the Christian Church. Edited by Henry Bettenson and Chris Maunder. Third ed. Oxford: Oxford University Press, 1999.

Giles, Kevin. *The Trinity and Subordinationism: The Doctrine of God and the Contemporary Gender Debate.* Downers Grove, IL: InterVarsity Press, 2002.

González, Justo L. *The Story of Christianity: Volume I: The Early Church to the Dawn of the Reformation.* San Francisco, CA: Harper Collins, 1984.

Grenz, Stanley J. *Rediscovering the Triune God: The Trinity in Contemporary Theology.* Minneapolis, MN: Fortress Press, 2004.

Grenz, Stanley J. *Theology for the Community of God.* Grand Rapids, Mich.: W.B. Eerdmans, 2000.

Grenz, Stanley J., and Denise Muir Kjesbo. *Women in the Church: A Biblical Theology of Women in Ministry*. Downers Grove, IL: InterVarsity Press, 1995.

Gunton, Colin E. "And in One Lord Jesus Christ ... Begotten Not Made." *Pro Ecclesia* 10, no. 3 (2001).

Gunton, Colin E. *The Promise of Trinitarian Theology*. New York, NY: T&T Clark Ltd, 2006.

Jacobsen, Douglas, and Rodney J. Sawatsky. *Gracious Christianity: Living the Love We Profess*. Grand Rapids, MI: Baker Academic, 2006.

Jenson, Robert W. *The Triune Identity*. Eugene, OR: Wipf and Stock, 2002.

Johnson, Elizabeth A. *She Who Is: The Mystery of God in Feminist Theological Discourse*. New York, NY: Crossroad Publishing Company, 1992.

Keener, Craig S. "Is Subordination Within the Trinity Really Heresy? A Study of John 5:18 in Context." *Trinity Journal* 20, no. 1 (1999): 39–51.

Kovach, Stephen D., and Peter R. Schemm, Jr. "A Defense of the Doctrine of the Eternal Subordination of the Son." *Journal of the Evangelical Theological Society* 42, no. 3 (1999): 461–76.

LaCugna, Catherine Mowry. *God for Us: The Trinity and Christian Life*. San Francisco, CA: Harper Collins, 1993.

Migliore, Daniel. *Faith Seeking Understanding: An Introduction to Christian Theology*. Grand Rapids, MI: Eerdman's, 2004.

Molnar, Paul D. *Divine Freedom and the Immanent Trinity: In Dialogue With Karl Barth and Contemporary Theology*. New York, NY: T&T Clark, 2002.

Moltmann, Jürgen. "The Fellowship of the Holy Spirit." *The Fellowship of the Holy Spirit—Trinitarian Pneumatology* 37, no. 3 (1984): 287–300.

Moltmann, Jürgen. *The Trinity and the Kingdom: The Doctrine of God*. Fortress Press ed. Minneapolis, MN: Fortress Press, 1993.

Moody, Dale. "God's Only Son: The Translation of John 3:16 in the RSV." *Journal of Biblical Literature* 72, no. 4 (1953): 213–19.

Newbigin, Leslie. *The Gospel in a Pluralist Society.* Grand Rapids, MI: W.B. Eerdmans, 1989.

Norris, Richard. "Trinity." In *The Holy Spirit: Classic and Contemporary Readings*, edited by Eugene F. Rogers. Chichester, West Sussex, UK: Wiley-Blackwell, 2009.

Peters, Ted. *God as Trinity: Relationality and Temporality in Divine Life.* Louisville, KY: Westminster John Knox Press, 1993.

Rahner, Karl. *The Trinity.* Translated by Joseph Donceel. New York, NY: Herder and Herder, 1970.

Roberts, R.L. "The Rendering of 'Only Begotten' In John 3:16." *Restoration Quarterly* 16, no. 1 (1973): 2–22.

Ross, Hugh. *Beyond the Cosmos.* Colorado Springs, CO: NavPress, 1999.

Speel, Charles J. "The Disappearance of Christianity From North Africa in the Wake of the Rise of Islam." *Church History* 29, no. 4 (1960): 379–97.

The Holy Spirit: Classic and Contemporary Readings. Edited by Eugene F. Rogers Jr. West Sussex, UK: Wiley-Blackwell, 2009.

Torrance, Thomas F. *The Christian Doctrine of God: One Being Three Persons.* New York, NY: T&T Clark, 1996.

Volf, Miroslav. *After Our Likeness: The Church as the Image of the Trinity*, Sacra Doctrina. Grand Rapids, MI: William B. Eerdmans, 1998.

Walton, John H. *The Lost World of Genesis One.* Downers Grove, IL: InterVarsity Press, 2010.

Zizioulas, John. *Being as Communion: Studies in Personhood and the Church*, Contemporary Greek Theologians. Crestwood, N.Y.: St. Vladimir's Seminary Press, 1985.

Made in the USA
San Bernardino, CA
30 December 2018